Astley Green Colliery

Compiled & Edited by Dave Lane, & the Red Rose Steam Society

"End of shift". Astley Green Colliery c1933

d.lane@btinternet.com

Second Edition January 2008

First Published   *January 2008*
Second Edition   *July 2008*

Published & Distributed Lulu
www.lulu.com

© *Dave Lane 2008*

The right of Dave Lane to be identified as the author of this work has been asserted in accordance with the UK Copyright, Design & Patents Act 1988

All rights reserved. No part of this publication may be reproduced, stored in a retrieval system, or transmitted, in any form or by any means, electronic, mechanical, photocopying, recording or otherwise, without the prior permission of the publishers.

ISBN 978-1-4092-2066-4

Printed in 12 pt Times New Roman font.

Frontispiece: Astley Green Colliery c1933
Front cover: Astley Green Colliery 1990's

CONTENTS

Preface   5

Introduction and History   7

The Museum   111

No 1 Engine   114

Transport at Astley Green   143

Demolition photographs   152

Colliery Facts in 1967   157

Red Rose Steam Society   162

List of Surface Workers at closure 164

Facts & Figures   170

Appendix   171

Manchester Collieries Ltd.

Producers and Distributors of

Quality Coals

Head Sales Office:

Arkwright House,
Parsonage, Manchester, 3.

Telephone: BLAckfriars 8633.   Telegrams: "Fuel Manchester."

Preface.

Much of the history of Astley Green Colliery has been written down over the past 15 years by present and past members of the Red Rose Steam Society, booklets have been written about the subject, web sites produced and talks have been given to interested parties.

This publication is an attempt to bring together all the known information and put it together in book form to provide a factual description of the coal mine of Astley Green for any interested reader.

When I volunteered to compile and publish this book, I found that a vast amount of written material had already been accumulated and written about the colliery by others. Although this book is technically "authored" by myself, by far the bulk of the information contained within it, is the work of others with **Graham Isherwood** being the major contributor. On many occasions other peoples writings have been used verbatim in this publication, with only a few alterations being made. There is no point in rewriting what has already been written!

Although the book generally follows a chronological order, extra articles have been slotted in as I researched further archived material.

The bulk of the illustrations in this publication are taken from the archives of the Red Rose Steam Society at Astley Green. Occasionally a photograph other than from the archives has been used and these will be indicated as such and the copyright owners listed in the appendix.

Where text has been used which has not been written by the author and where the original authors are known, they are fully acknowledged in the appendix along with everyone else who has provided information to make this book possible. If anyone feels they have been "missed out", please contact me at d.lane@btinternet.com so that future editions of this book can be amended.

Dave Lane
January 2008

Astley Green Colliery Museum.

Opening times

Opening Times:
Sunday: 1.00 pm to 5.00 pm
Tuesday: 1.00 pm to 5.00 pm
Thursday: 1.00 pm to 5.00 pm
Closed:
Christmas Day and Boxing Day
Group Visits:
The site can be opened at other times by prior arrangement for school parties and other interested groups. See the Contacting Us page for contact details. Please go to http://www.agcm.org.uk/schoolvisit.pdf to view or download a suggested itinerary for school groups.
Location:
Higher Green Lane,
Astley Green,
Tyldesley,
Lancashire.
Directions:
At the traffic lights south west of Boothstown, take the turning to Higher Green. Proceed down Higher Green Lane to the small grassed area, on the left. Immediately after this area turn left. The gates to the museum are directly ahead.

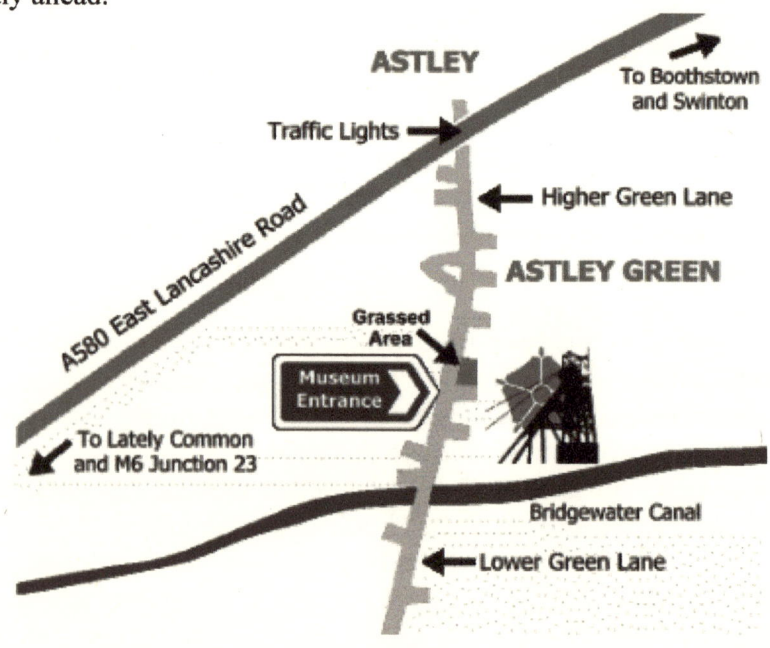

INTRODUCTION

Astley Green Colliery is situated 3 miles east of Leigh and 8 miles west of Manchester, about 500 yards to the South of the East Lancashire Road. Today, all that can be seen of this once thriving concern is the Engine House of its No.1 Shaft, the Shaft Headgear, and two other buildings.

Visitors to the site often look around and say "Was there a colliery here?" so effective has been the land reclamation. It is only through good fortune that anything remains at all. For Astley has some claims to fame, the remaining engine house contains what was and now is, one of the largest steam winding engines ever to have been installed in this country and certainly the largest built and erected in Lancashire.

At the eleventh hour when the colliery closed in 1970 and the demolition contractors moved in, far sighted officials of Lancashire County Council and prominent museum representatives in the North West persuaded the N.C.B. to leave the engine alone along with its headgear and outbuildings. Unfortunately at the time, apart from boarding up the windows that was all that was done and so the engine remained locked away, prey to vandals and the weather alike until some ten years later a group of steam engine enthusiasts were given permission to move onto the site in the hope that eventually a museum of some kind might be developed around the old pit head.

A Herculean task confronted the group, a task still going on to restore the old winding engine to some semblance of its former dignity and beauty.

The engine house was restored, glazed and services laid on by the generous hand of the then Greater Manchester Council. Even so, it is difficult for many to imagine what it must have been like when the engine was an essential part of the pit. This publication tells the story of the pit, and its equipment, from its beginnings in 1908 up to the final closure of 1970 plus a few comments about the present day.

No 1 pit and engine house. Both these structures are still intact although the associated chimney has been demolished. No 2 pit is visible at the left of the photo.

Aerial view of Astley Green 1963. The main gate is on the right.

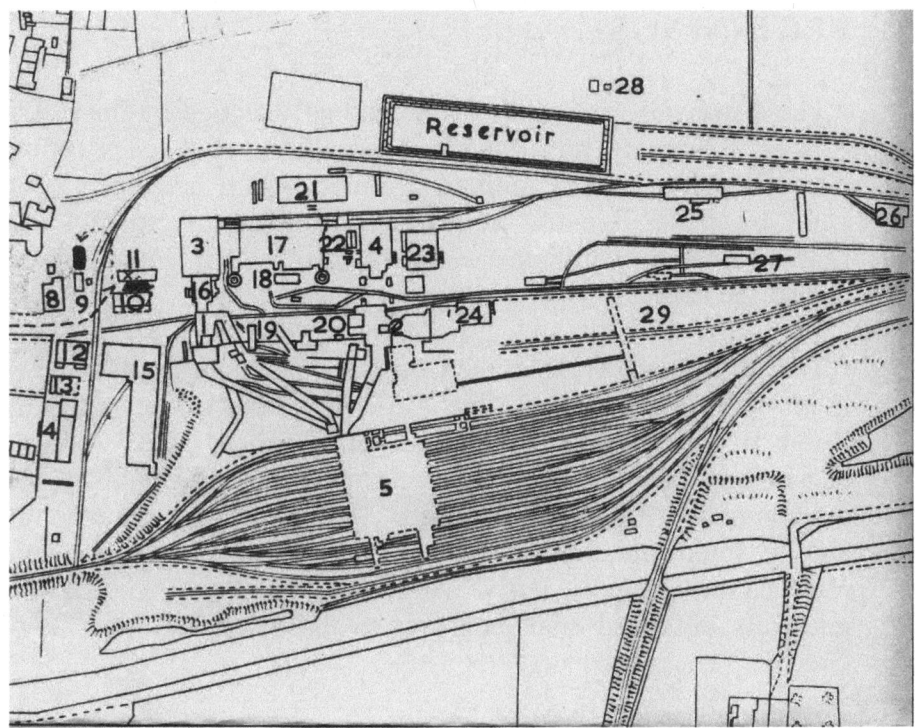

1 - No 1 Shaft
2 - No 2 Shaft
3 - No 1 Winding Engine
4 - No 2 Winding Engine
5 – Screens
6 - Pithead Baths
7 – Canteen
8 - General Offices
9 - Time & Weigh Office
10 – Lamproom
11 - Electricians
12 - Garage
13 - Oil Stores
14 - Workshops
15 - Workshops & Stores
16 - Capstan House
17 - Boiler House
18 - Pulveriser Plant
19 - Mortar Mill
20 - Powder Magazine

21 – Power House
22 – Pump House
23 – Compressor House
24 – Fan House
25 – Loco Shed
26 – Loco Shed
27 – Sand Stores
28 – Powder Magazine
29 – Timber Stores Yard
x - Power Plant

BEGINNINGS

The Astley Green Colliery was originally owned by the Pilkington Colliery Company, an offshoot of the Clifton & Kersley (nowadays spelt Kearsley) Coal Company Limited which had been set up in 1867 by the Pilkington and Evans brothers of St. Helens. The Limited Liability Company was set up on the 31st. July 1885 with an authorised capital of £400,000 in £10 shares.

The Collieries owned by the Company included Wet Earth, Spindle Point, Outwood, Newtown, Moss (Unity Brook), Manor (Kearsley), Robin Hood and Botany Bay (Clifton). Of these Moss, Robin Hood and Botany Bay had already closed by 1900, and Manor by 1905 so the company's older collieries in the Irwell valley were reaching the elderly stage and their closure was in sight when their workable reserves ran out in the early 1900's. Attention was then drawn to the relatively untapped coal measures to the south and west at Astley Green.

The coal seams which outcropped around Tyldesley and to the north dip down in a southerly direction at approximately 1 in 5. Many of the working collieries lay where the main seams were only at a shallow depth beneath the surface, extending southwards and deeper as the local resources of coal became exhausted.

The coal could be worked down dip with respect to the access points in the shafts (insets) and thus require haulage up towards the shaft, or it could be worked to the rise above the shaft inset position and thus be easily lowered to the roadways which fed the shaft. At Astley, much further to the south than any of the existing collieries, the coal seams were deeper and lay beneath a thick layer of alluvial deposits and sandstones known to contain water and any attempt to work them would require a deep and expensive shaft to be sunk before any coal could be got.

There had also been resistance from the Bridgewater Canal owners to mining in the vicinity of the canal. A Liverpool firm got as far as sinking a trial borehole 1713ft. deep about 3/4 mile to the south of the eventual colliery site between 1899 and 1901 but this met with such prodigious quantities of water that it was abandoned. The borehole reached the Coal Measures but stopped short of the first workable seam (Worsley 4ft.). Eleven years later when Astley was being sunk, it was still visibly gushing water to the surface.

The Pilkington brothers were not deterred, however, and by 1908 agreements had been reached with the various landowners and work began on the colliery site, just to the north of the Bridgewater Canal in the part of Astley known as Higher Green.

Two shafts were to be sunk, some 90 yards apart as had become the practice, the intention being to develop the RAMS (1752ft.) and TRENCHERBONE (2481ft.) coal seams in an area bounded by the Mosley Common Colliery to the east, the Parsonage and Bedford Collieries to the west, and the Nook, Gin, St. Georges and Cleworth Hall Collieries to the north.

To the south the site was bounded by a downthrow fault known as the Lions Bridge Fault. It was thought that this fault would throw the Rams, Binn, Doe, and Crombouke seams down opposite the horizon of the Trencherbone and Victoria seams to the north of the fault. In consequence the No.2, or east, shaft was intended to wind the Rams coal (north of the fault), and thereafter become the main man-riding and ventilation shaft with all the output being wound up the No.1 shaft which was to be equipped appropriately.

No. 1 shaft was designated the downcast shaft, fresh air was to be drawn down it and passed around the workings to the foot of the No. 2 shaft, the upcast shaft whose headgear would have to be enclosed and connected to a ventilation fan by a passage called the fan drift. Any coal raised by this shaft would have to pass through air locks both at the pit bank and the insets so as not to short-circuit the air currents. Hence the intention to use the No. 1 shaft for all coal raising once the colliery was properly started.

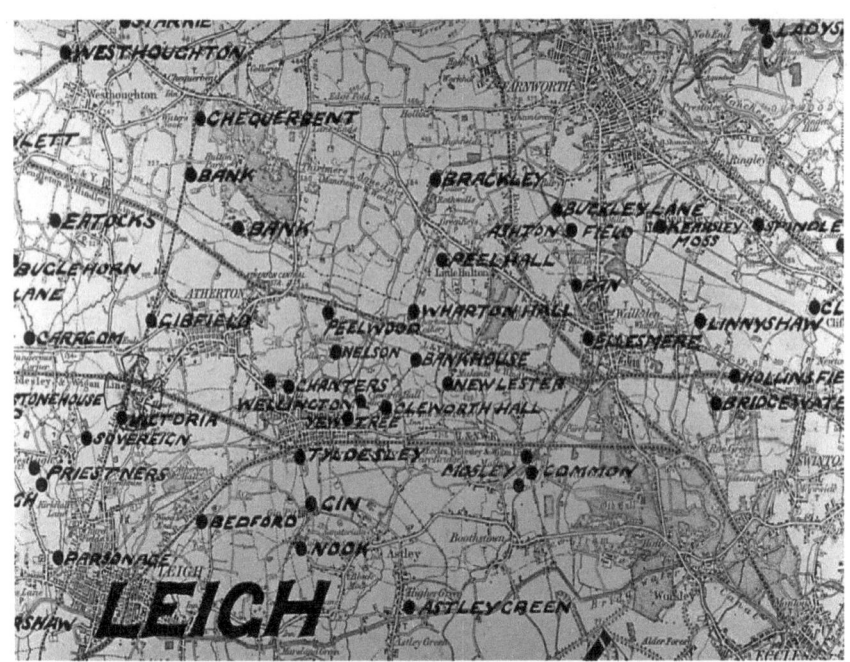

Collieries adjacent to the north of Astley Green

The cover of the Dec 1935 issue of Carbon, the house magazine of Manchester Collieries.

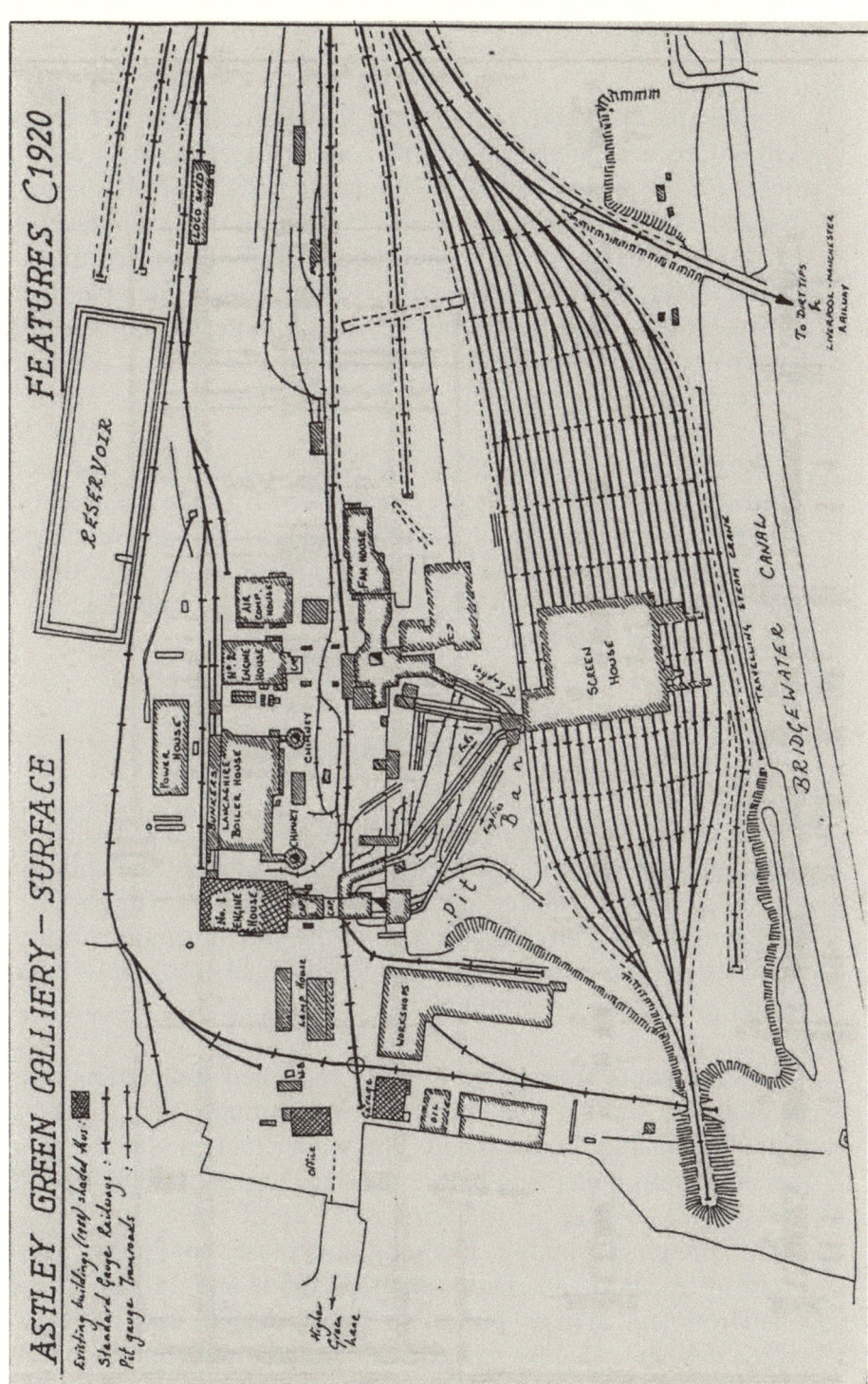

GEOLOGY

Unlike the exposed coalfield to the north, the coal measures at Astley Green lie under sandstones and marl of Permian age. These rocks are themselves overlain by glacial drift. From the surface the first 30ft. is stiff clay followed by 99ft 4in of unconsolidated glacial drift containing water and quicksand. The following Permian rocks have a thickness of 310ft 7in and also contain considerable quantities of water. Below the Permian lies the Middle Coal Measures (the Upper Coal Measures having been eroded away before deposition of the Permian).

The first seam worked was the Worsley Four Feet at a depth of 772ft 4in followed by 10 other seams down to the Trencherbone at 2481ft. The seams dip to the south at about 1 in 5 and outcrop to the north in Tyldesley where coal mining is recorded in the 15th century. The coalfield is broken by NW-SE and E-W faults which often created natural boundaries to the collieries.

THE SINKING

Fortunately, a series of photographs taken on the surface during sinking operations and during the first few years of the colliery's life give a vivid picture of the site and its development. The earliest shots were concerned with the setting up of the sinking engine for the No.1 shaft, its capstan winch, which was immediately in front of it, and the building up of the brick collar.

Several eminent engineers were consulted concerning the best method of sinking the shafts down through the water-bearing unstable strata to the rockhead. The main problem was the danger of the shaft walls collapsing before the shaft lining could be installed.

The principal sinking methods for these conditions were the Freezing method, the Drop Shaft method, and Piling. The Kind-Chaudron and similar boring methods, which used a huge "bit" which descended under its own weight were not suitable because of the loose nature of the ground, the unsupported sides of the shaft being unstable.

The Freezing method consisted of boring a series of holes outside the circle of the intended shaft. These were fitted with pipes through which a freezing liquid (such as brine) was circulated, freezing the ground around them and allowing the shaft site to be excavated.

This process tended to be expensive due to the cost of the equipment for supplying the freezing solution and the boring of the freezing holes. It had first been used in Britain in the Durham Coalfield at Washington Colliery in 1901.

The Dropshaft or Sinking Drum Process involved forcing an iron cylinder through the ground and excavating within it. Although the Germans had used this method, it was new to Britain. It was considered that the German firm of Haniel & Lueg in Dusseldorf had expertise in the latter two methods and a visit was made to Germany to discuss the project with Herr Reimer, the doyen of difficult shaft sinking. His book "Shaft Sinking in Difficult Cases" remains a classic on the subject. Reimer was emphatic in his preference for the freezing process, but as this was considered too expensive, it was decided to go for the Dropshaft method, and Haniel & Lueg undertook to supply the necessary equipment and materials. It is probable that they also managed the actual shaft sinking down to the end of the tubbing.

A diary note for 2nd April 1909 states that "10 unemployed men came form Manchester to work as sinkers but only 3 returned to work the following day"! The Dropshaft sinking method uses cylinders of cast iron (tubbing) which are made of a number of segments bolted together. The tubbing is forced into the ground by hydraulic jacks thereby providing a shield for the sinkers to excavate the shaft. Further cylinders of tubbing are attached and pushed down as the sinking proceeds.

The sequence of operations was to commence with the construction of a massive thrust pillar on the surface above the shaft. This large mass of 2200 tons was required to resist the force of the jacks which would be pushing the iron tubbing down the shaft. Once the pillar was complete and the jacks installed the Drop Shaft method would be used to sink through the 100ft. of glacial drift.

The next 310ft. of sandstones were stable but very wet and the shaft lining would be continued but the ground would be first excavated and the tubbing segments lowered down the shaft and then bolted up to the previous section. The remainder of the shaft through the Coal Measures would be brick lined.

Anticipating water problems when sinking through the glacial drift, in 1907 the Clifton & Kersley Coal Co. Ltd. sank a borehole 2ft. diameter and 30 feet from the centre of the intended No.1 shaft. This was intended to be used for pumping water away from the sinking operations. Unfortunately, the contractor responsible for the borehole buckled the metal lining being fitted to the borehole. During the four months taken to correct this problem unbeknown to all concerned, the pumping was creating a cavity about 100ft. below the surface.

This was to have serious consequences during the sinking proper. Work began in earnest on site early in 1908, the foundations were laid for the sinking engine houses and construction of the other essential buildings began.

Cutting the First Sod

The Cutting of the First Sod Ceremony to celebrate the start of sinking of No.1 shaft took place on May 7th. 1908, Lady Pilkington doing the honours. This was followed by the construction on the cleared surface of a temporary wooden ring in which 26 equi-distant holes were bored on a diameter of 27ft.6ins. Brickwork was then built up on this to an inside diameter of 24ft. 11ins., 5ft. high, with a second wooden ring on top. Bolts 1.5ins. in diameter and 6ft. long were pushed through the holes in the two rings and into the underlying clay. A reinforced concrete block 50ft across and 3.5ft thick was then laid around the brickwork.

Another view of the "first sod" ceremony. May 7th 1908

Sinking into the clay commenced on May 11th. A bricking platform was placed in position round the bottom of the shaft when the depth reached 17 feet. Construction of a brick collar on the concrete platform, and a brick pillar within the shaft then commenced, the pillar being reinforced by extensions to the original bolts as required.

All construction lifting at this stage was carried out by a long jib crane to avoid any disturbance to the growing pillar which might cause it to stray from the vertical, as it would form the guide through which the cast iron tubbing of the shaft would be forced downwards.

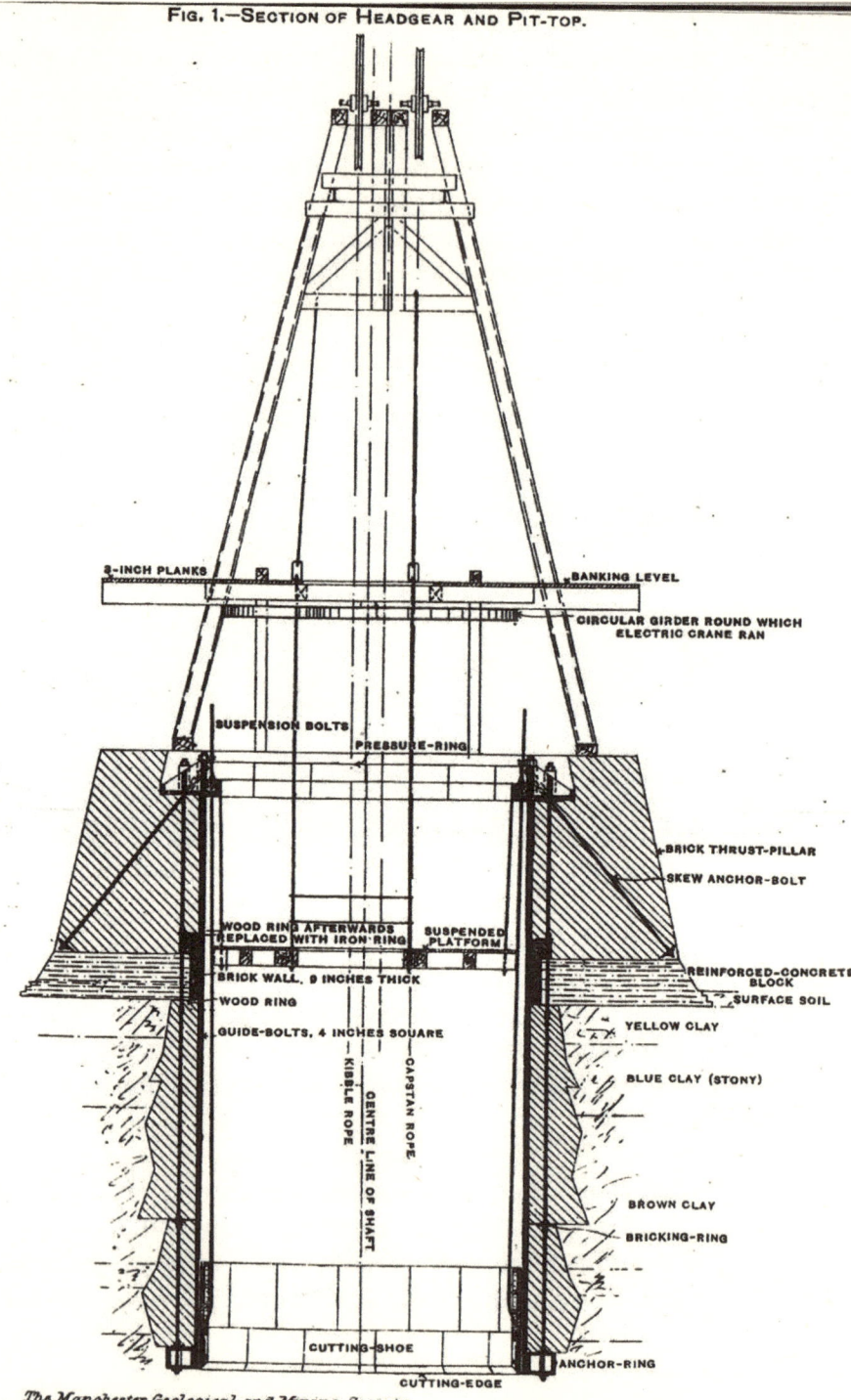

Fig. 1.—Section of Headgear and Pit-top.

When the 25ft. level was reached, a cast iron Anchor-ring was laid, and connected by 4ins. bolts to a second Pressure-ring at the top of the collar. The Pressure-ring was also locked into the collar by skew bolts, rendering the whole into a single solid mass. The weight of the whole collar and pillar amounted to 2200 tons, the anchor-ring weighing 25 tons and the pressure ring 45 tons. Hydraulic jacks were then hung from the pressure ring. These were 6ins. diameter by 22ins. stroke and were fed from a steam driven pump via an accumulator.

Construction of No 1 brick pillar. June 1908

Water was supplied at a maximum pressure of 5 tons per square inch, giving each jack a force of 150 tons over its stroke. Thus the total force exerted by the jacks amounted to 1800 tons hence the massive brickwork!

Drop Shaft

With the sinking engines ready, it only required the construction of the sinking headgear and the necessary pulleys and supports before sinking proper could begin. The cast-iron tubbing to be used was heavy, each segment was 3ins. thick, 5ft. deep and weighed 2 tons. As the stroke of the jacks was less than the depth of a ring of tubbing, two shorter make-up rings were used at the surface until each ring of tubbing had been forced down sufficiently to place the next on top of it. At the bottom of the tubbing was the Cutting Shoe which would be repeatedly forced into the ground by the jacks thereby forming a shield for the shaft excavation to proceed safely.

To handle the tubbing, a circular rail was laid around the top of the shaft, and H-section girders laid to run on these. This structure supported an electric crane worked by two motors whose task it was to manoeuvre the plates into position beneath the jacks. These tubbing segments had a smooth outer side to follow the brick pillar, there being lugs on the inside to bolt them together. Lead sheet and washers were used in the joints and under the bolts as a gasket to make the tubbing water tight (water pressures up to 100psi were recorded).

At a depth of 11ft. 5in below the pressure ring was the bricking scaffold, which supported the men working on the tubbing etc. This had a central hole 8ft. square to allow the hoppit or kibble to pass through. Also suspended below this were the pumps to remove water from the shaft. These were of the Ellison Pulsometer type and were essential once the shaft bottom was below the water table which lay about 18 ft. below the surface. The water was conducted over the shaft collar in a large pipe which discharged into wooden troughs laid across the ground towards the canal. The water flow exceeded 15000 gallons an hour at times.

No 1 brick collar under construction 1908

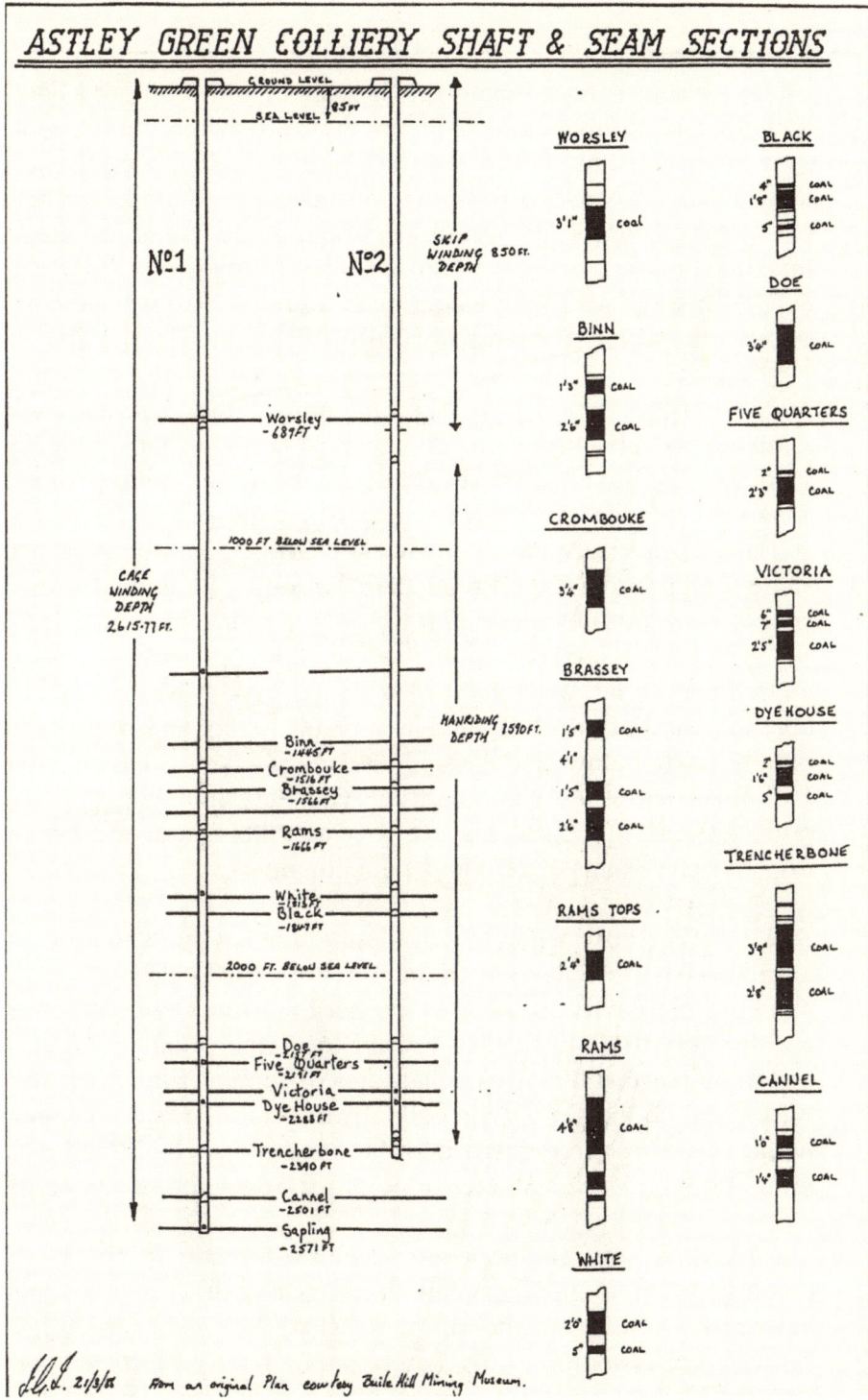

Quicksand

The sinking proper began on September 8th 1908 and continued without any trouble until October the 18th when, with the cutting shoe about 14ft. 6in below the shaft bottom as had been the practise, it would not advance any further despite the full force of the jacks. On investigation, sand was found to have risen some 10 feet above the shaft bottom. This was too soft for the men to work and so the hoppit was replaced with a contractor's grab which was able to work through the water which now had risen above the sand.

The inrush of sand had blocked the pumps and these had had to be removed for cleaning. The grab was successful and many tons of sand were removed from the shaft, enabling the cutting shoe to be advanced another 22ins. However, when the pumps were restored and the water cleared away again on October 21st, the sand was still some 9 feet above the original shaft bottom! The grab was therefore kept in work until October 25th when the ground became more solid.

On making an examination, a large cavity was found on the borehole side of the shaft, and as a result sand was being washed up into it from below and behind the cutting shoe, which was now 16ft.4ins. below the shaft bottom. The only immediate solution to protect the shaft was to place a ring of tubbing outside the sinking ring and place bags of cement against them.

The surface now began to subside into the cavity, whose origin was ascribed to the problems with the borehole, the buckling of the lining allowing the cavity to form in the period while the obstruction was cut through. The subsidence caused the brick pillar to begin to tilt, and to help arrest this, large quantities of tubbing and other ironwork were hung on the side of the collar away from the borehole and thick liquid cement poured down into the borehole by night and day. The ground fell under the concrete block by 2.5 feet and had to be filled.

While this was going on all haste was made to try to get the tubbing down to the Permian marls where it could be anchored before the effects of the tilting caused the anchor bolts to bind against the tubbing rings and prevent any further progress. Fortunately fate was with them and the cutting shoe entered the marls on November 13th. 1908. To be safe, the cutting shoe was forced further down until the 26th of November.

Temporary pithead at No 1 shaft

The effect of the tilting was seen when the 4-inch anchor bolts were found to have been bent nearly eight inches out of the vertical in 28 feet depth. At the same time, when the shaft bottom was cut from beneath the cutting shoe, the tubbing was found to be self supporting, despite its 514 ton weight.

The hydraulic jacks, their connections and the anchor ring were removed to be used at the No.2 shaft, and the upper layers of tubbing above the water table within the brick pillar were also removed. It had been intended to re-use the cutting shoe and pressure ring also, but in view of the problems, it was decided to retain the pressure ring to reinforce the pillar and collar.

It was also felt safest to leave the cutting shoe in place rather than risk any disturbance to the strata by removing it. As the rest of the tubbing would hang from the cutting shoe already in place, the electric crane, H beams and rail were also removed to the No.2 sinking.

No 1 pressure ring during the sinking. August 1908

Hydraulic jacks in position for sinking. August 1908

Underhanging Tubbing

The headframe was then altered to handle the tubbing rings and lower them down the shaft, the Pulsometer pumps were replaced by an Evans sinking pump capable of the full lift to the surface in one stage rather than the several which had been needed with the Pulsometers whose intermediate tanks had added to the obstructions in the shaft.

To join the underhung tubbing to the cutting shoe, an unforeseen event, 1 inch thick boiler plate was fastened round the outside of the cutting shoe and an inner ring attached from which a special ring of tubbing was suspended by 1 7/16ins. diameter bolts. Half inch thick wooden sheeting was fixed between the tubbing ring and the bottom edge of the cutting shoe.

Both temporary pitheads at Astley Green Colliery viewed from the South with No 1 pit on the left side of the photo. The wagons visible were used for tipping on the pit bank.

The tubbing used below the cutting shoe was still referred to by the sinkers as "German" tubbing, even though it had cast lugs on the outside to help it key into the cement (in other words it was "English" tubbing) because it was supplied by Haniel and Lueg. Above the cutting shoe, the inside diameter of the tubbing was 23 feet, while below it it was to be 21 feet. The tubbing to the cutting shoe was found to be less than 4 inches out of the vertical despite all the problems, and conical joint rings were made to centre the rest of the shaft.

Sinkers fitting underhanging tubbing – this photo may NOT have been taken at Astley Green.

Water

To avoid further dangers, a borehole was driven ahead of the bottom of the shaft to warn of water, but it was not until after the 10th. March 1909 at a depth of 283 feet from the surface that the Evans pump was put into action. Up to that time the hoppit had been sufficient to bale out the water. At 292 feet a feeder of water was struck, bringing the make of water in the shaft to 30,000 gallons per hour. This was handled after much difficulty by placing a Vee ring at 303 feet on pitch pine wedges to stop the water flowing down behind the tubbing.

The water from above the Vee ring was conducted down the inside of the shaft in 1.5ins. pipes to the intake of the sinking pump. Cement grout was then poured through oblique holes in the tubbing below the Vee ring, the Vee ring and water diversion giving the cement time to set hard. When it was set, the pipes could be removed and the holes plugged. By these methods the make of water was reduced to under 5000 gallons per hour.

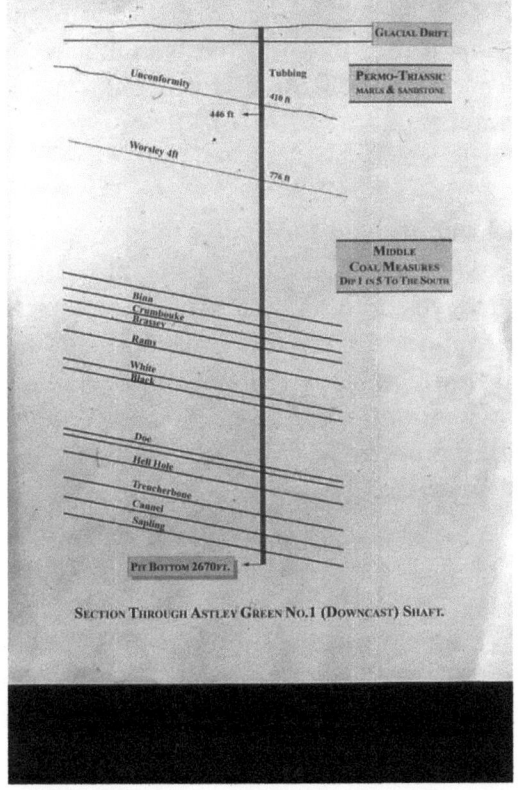

Section Through Astley Green No.1 (Downcast) Shaft.

At 379 feet a second feeder of 25,000 gallons per hour was dealt with successfully by the same method, but only after severe difficulty. However this was the last major feeder to be contended with in the sinking. Despite the tubbing having been made to follow very close to the pit bottom and thus being exposed to the blasting, no tubbing was damaged in the process.

A true English wedging curb was laid after the last of the sandstones had been passed, the make of water by this time only amounting to 7,000 gallons per hour. The idea being to form a seal with the surrounding rock so that no water could enter the shaft. This would allow conventional brick lining to be used for the rest of the depth. The last ring of tubbing immediately above it was made with an especially strong flange to resist the wedging.

The wedging curb was laid at a depth of 446ft. 2ins. on a dark shale on one side and a strong rocky warrant on the other. This was not felt to be the best foundation.

The curb was laid on September 9th 1909 and keyed up with cement on September the 15th, stout timber wedges having been forced between it and the tubbing ring until the full force of a hammer could not drive them any further. The water was pumped from behind the tubbing as already described, until September the 24th, when it was felt that the cement would have set well enough.

Thus the pipes were removed, the holes plugged and a pressure gauge fitted. Unfortunately the pressure rose rapidly to 40 p.s.i. at which point it spurted out through weak places in the joints of the tubbing and under the wedging curb! Clearly, the wedging was not a success, so the tubbing was continued down further and a second wedging curb laid on October 28th 1909 on flaggy rock some 12ft.10ins below the first curb.

The pumping this time was continued for longer to give the cement more time to set. Pumping was halted on November 28th at 10 a.m.. By 4 p.m. the pressure had risen to 60 p.s.i. and by the 3rd of December it was 100 p.s.i. and once again the joints sprung leaks but not as badly as before. Further cement grout was poured into place behind the tubbing and it was found that the pressure was regulated by the quantity of water being pumped at No.2 pit.

Coal

Sinking below the wedging curb then continued, but with conventional brick lining of the shaft. Richard Davis & Son was given the contract for sinking below the tubbing on 12th January 1910. However, there was a dispute later in the year and the contract was terminated on 13th October when No.1 shaft was at a depth of 461 yards.

An account for the shaft sinking (excluding materials) below the tubbing shows a cost of £11/10/9 per yard for No.1 shaft (against a contract price of £15/11/6 per yard), the main expenses being sinkers' wages at £7917, pumping £606, and explosives £757. It is not clear whether Davis and Son was reinstated after the dispute although no other contractor is mentioned and only one contract price is stated.

The Worsley 4ft. coal seam was reached on April 7th 1910 at a depth of 772ft. 4ins., while sinking was completed by the end of 1912 through the Crombouke (1602 ft.), Rams (1752 ft.), Trencherbone (2481 ft.) and Cannel seams to an absolute pit bottom 2670 feet below the surface. References at the time make it clear that this was not the final intended bottom, and it was hoped to eventually sink deeper still to the Arley seam. This was, however, never to be fulfilled.

It was notable that despite all the difficulties and the heavy and dangerous work, there was no loss of life during the shaft sinking.

CONSTRUCTION

1908

Work on the engine house for the No.1 shaft sinking engine was started early in 1908 together with the Lamp Room, Sinkers' Cabin, and Boiler House. Bricks were initially brought to the site from the Company's brickworks at Newtown, but by March 1908 the brickworks on site was operational and supplied most of the bricks from that date.

One of the first Yates & Thom boilers being installed. 1909

By August 1908, four of the large Lancashire-type boilers had been set up and were being hand fired in the open, coal being shovelled out of wagons on to the ground for stoking. Only a rough timber shelter had been erected to shield the stokers from the elements. At least one other boiler, from Yates & Thom of Blackburn, was on site and was lying close by the others on its side, awaiting erection.

The tubbing rings and coal for the boilers appear to have been brought to the site by the Bridgewater Canal in barges. The coal was in boxes which were lifted out of the barges by crane and loaded onto standard gauge wagons which ran around the site. Latterly the process was reversed when the colliery was in production!

Photo of the pit sinkers in front of the boilers. 1909

1909

By February 1909, the sinking headframe was being erected over the No.1 shaft and a reciprocating type air compressor was being erected in a new building to the east of the No.2 shaft sinking engine.

Both temporary wooden headframes were complete and in use by April 1909, spoil from the shafts being discharged from the bank level onto dumb-buffered side-tipping wagons which were being used to build up the pitbank to the south of the shafts and between them and the canal. The pitbank was by this time about half the height of the shaft collar.

In accordance with the original plan, the No.1 shaft was to be equipped with an engine large enough to handle the whole of the output of the colliery. The engine contracts for both No.1 and No.2 winding engines were let to Yates & Thom of the Canal Ironworks, Blackburn, who had also supplied the initial boilers to the site.

The ancillary gear was contracted out to Fraser & Chalmers of Erith, Kent. There is some doubt as to whether, in fact, F. & C. actually supplied the gear direct, or sub-contracted it out to the firm of N.L.King of Nailsworth, Glos., who supplied these for engines not of F. & C.'s own manufacture.

Temporary No 1 headgear as seen from No 2. April 1909

The boiler house was completed by August 1909, or at least completed enough for the then existing boiler set. There were now eight boilers, five in work at any one time. The flue gases were exhausted either directly to the 156ft. high western chimney stack, or via a bank of Green's Economisers.

The firing floor had by now been covered over with a corrugated iron shelter for its full length, while on the opposite side of the firing aisle from the boilers a brickwork bunker arrangement allowed wagons to discharge their coal directly into the bunkers from the track. The following month saw the No.1 engine house built up to working floor level, so the work of erection of the engine could commence.

1910

The No.1 Engine house was the main building project from then on; the roof girders were being placed in December 1910, the travelling crane of 20 ton capacity which ran along the top of the walls already being in position and in use handling the various engine parts. The first record of coal being mined is May 1910 when 63 tons of Worsley 4ft. were burnt on the boilers.

Installation of the Bellis & Morcom 220Kw generator on the brick pier. 1909

1911

April 1911 brought the pitbank up to the height of the brick collar and the permanent headframe for the No.1 shaft was being erected by the firm of Head Wrightson & Co. of Stockton on Tees around the sinking headframe, thus allowing the work in the shaft to go on unimpeded. Behind the boiler house, work had begun on the power house, a Bellis & Morcom steam driven generator being set up on its brickwork pier in July, while in No.1 engine house, erection was proceeding apace.

A photograph taken in September 1911 shows all the auxiliaries (brake engine, reverser etc.) to be in place in front of the drum. The drum itself was unlagged, there was, as yet, no floor to the engine house and whilst the trunk guides were in place, the cranks and the various rods were not. By July 1912, all was ready, the engine house and its massive occupant were complete, as was the headgear. The headgear is of lattice steel construction, the sheaves being supported some 98 feet above the ground. The sheaves are 20 ft. in diameter and the whole frame weighed 120 tons.

No 1 headgear under construction. 1911

One photograph of the final building operations shows the headgear standing naked to the air, the sinking headframe finally absent from beneath it, the guide ropes for the cages hanging limply from its upperworks. Tramways can be seen undulating across the uneven surface of the pitbank from the lip of the shaft. These led towards the temporary screen by the No. 2 shaft. These were arranged at the southern edge of the pitbank, and discharged straight into standard gauge wagons alongside. The photographs also show the containers of coal ("boxes") on flat wagons ready to be taken to the wharf and transferred to canal barges.

Railway

Railway wagons could now reach the site directly from a main line railway, the London & North Western's line across Chat Moss from Manchester to Liverpool. The laying of this mineral line across the Astley peat bog had had its own share of problems, the bog being up to 28 feet deep in places. The solution had been to lay the track on piles of brushwood in a manner very similar to that employed by George Stephenson when the Liverpool and Manchester Railway was originally constructed.

The colliery railway joined the main line by a triangular junction from which it plunged off directly northward towards Astley. It climbed a bridge over the Bridgewater Canal and swung eastwards toward the colliery sidings, from where reversal was needed to reach the colliery proper. At the extreme eastern end of the site the tracks swung north and then reversed again to a small canal wharf and raised tippler bank. This had originally served a tramway (Green's Tramway) from the Tyldesley collieries until the arrival of the London and North Western Railway in that town had taken the trade away.

Canal

The Duke of Bridgewater's Canal had been extended from Worsley to Leigh in 1799 and it was of course no coincidence that the colliery was built just to the north. A loading wharf was constructed for transferring coal from railway wagons to the boats. The coal was transported from the screens in boxes which were loaded into the Box Boats by steam crane. This was what we would refer to today as "containerisation" but it had already been established on the Bridgewater over 100 years earlier.

The boxes were made of wood strengthened with iron. The bottom had two hinged iron doors operated by a windlass mounted at the top of the box. A pawl and ratchet system both secured the doors and also allowed rapid discharge. Except for one notable exception all the box boats were horse drawn with two boats being pulled by one horse. A "captain" would steer the first boat and two boys would take turns steering the second boat or leading the horse. Much of the coal taken by canal went to the power stations at Trafford Park and Stretford. The unique motorised box boat "Fred" was saved for preservation but unfortunately was later destroyed by vandels.

After the demise of the box boats, coal was still transported by canal in barges. *Coal News* in December 1968 reported that coal from Astley Green was taken by rail to Boothstown tippler where it was transferred to barges. Each barge carried 50tons and was taken to Stretford Power station where the coal was sucked out via a nine-inch pipe. At that time the 250-strong NCB fleet had been reduced to 27 boats, 14 of which were engaged in maintaining the canal banks.

Construction Costs
Engine House   £4,133
No.1 Winding Engine   £9,677

No.1 Shaft Sinking   £214 per yard with tubbing
                             £60 per yard brick lined
                             £87 per yard average
No.2 Shaft Sinking   £81 per yard average

Laying track to the tip on the pit bank circa 1909. Man on left of photo is T Gilman who later worked underground.

Head sinker in kibble. April 1909

Raising pulley wheel to top of No 1, note the steam crane. 1911

Number 1 engine house under construction. 3rd March 1911

No 1 engine crane with the roof under construction

A photo taken around 1912 of a group in front of the No 1 headgear. The original wooden headgear is still in place.

Laying track behind No 1 engine house. C1912

Capstan engines for No 1 under construction c 1908

No 2 headgear under construction.

No 2 headgear. Note the flag at half mast and the arch to connect with the fan

DEVELOPMENTS 1913-1928

As a new colliery, Astley received a number of official visits, especially in view of the difficulties that had attended the sinking - a description of which had been read by Messrs. Charles Pilkington and Percy L.Wood to the Manchester Geological and Mining Society in 1910 and which was repeated verbatim in the transactions of the Institute of Mining Engineers. These and subsequent occasions on which Astley was brought into the spotlight have enabled this account to be written.

Power

A visitor to the colliery in 1913 informs us that the winding engine exhausted into a Rateau Morison accumulator, this being situated at the western end of the power house. The latter contained a 220 kW Bellis & Morcom inverted vertical steam driven generator, a Musgrave Zoelly 400 kW mixed pressure steam turbine fed with steam from both the boiler house and also from a steam accumulator, and a Bellis & Morcom air compressor of 1000 cubic feet per minute capacity driven by a 200 h.p. motor. Both the generators provided 3-phase A.C. electricity at 2000 volts, 50 cycles.

With the development of the colliery, the electricity requirements had also increased and the power house eventually boasted a 2MW turbo-alternator by Metropolitan-Vickers and a 1MW mixed pressure turbine by Fraser & Chalmers which drove a Lancashire Dynamo & Crypto Co. alternator. The mixed pressure turbines were fed from a bank of Rateau-Morrison steam accumulators which took the exhaust from the winding engines and the fan engine at 5 p.s.i..

Compressed Air

Initially most of the underground machinery was powered by compressed air. The main compressor, to the east of the No.2 sinking engine house, was steam driven, manufactured by Ingersoll. The cross-compound engine, with steam cylinders of 17ins. and 38ins. in diameter and 42ins. stroke, supplied 3,000 cubic feet of air per minute from air cylinders 20.25ins and 32.25ins in diameter.

The reciprocating compressor house's initial capacity was increased by the addition of a second 2000 c.f.m. reciprocating compressor manufactured by Tilghman and electrically driven. This was accommodated by doubling the width of the compressor house.

No. 2 Engine

The No.2 shaft permanent winding engine, itself a cross compound type, had cylinders 36ins. and 60ins. in diameter with a stroke of 72ins. It was fitted with Corliss valves and Allens straight link motion. With a capacity of 254 tons per hour from 632 yards, this was half the size of the number one engine as befitted its role as man riding and materials haulage. It was on order from Yates and Thom before 1914, but owing to the outbreak of war, this was delayed and the original sinking engine was used to wind the shaft, a small pair of cages replacing the hoppit which had been used during the sinking.

Legend has it that the engine had already been constructed at Yates & Thom's works and broken down for transport when the word came to stop it, and so it remained throughout the war. This sort of story can be heard in connection with cotton mill engines, so it may well be true in this connection also. Certainly the N.C.B records refer to the date of construction of the No. 2 engine as being 1913, although erection did not occur until 1918-19 when the timber headgear of the No.2 shaft was also replaced by permanent steelwork.

A report in 1944 stated that the No.2 engine gave "rough winding" which was attributed to the compound arrangement of the cylinders. A proposal to convert the engine to a simple twin cylinder type had been rejected on grounds of cost.

Ventilation

To provide ventilation for the initial pit working, a Schiele electrically driven fan was installed close by the top of the No.2 shaft collar. This was 12 feet in diameter and driven by a 100 h.p. motor. The Schiele fan was supplanted in 1914-15 by a steam driven fan of the "Indestructible" type manufactured by Walker Bros. of Pagefield Ironworks, Wigan.

The fan was 28ft. in diameter and 9 feet wide. It was driven by one of Walker's own cross-compound steam engines with rope drive. The fan and engine houses were sited to the east of the No.2 shaft buildings and were capable of giving up to 700,000 cubic feet per minute against a head of 7ins water gauge, although the developing colliery required only a small part of that.

No. 1 shaft

At No.1 shaft, with its engine designed to handle the whole output of the colliery, the shaft arrangements were impressive. The two cages each had three decks and were designed to carry twelve tubs of coal, four on each deck. The tubs weighed 10 cwt. and had a maximum capacity of 15 cwt. of coal giving a total maximum load in the cage of of 15 tons. The total weight on the winding rope at the start of the wind was around 45 tons.

In order to start this load the winding drum on the engine was shaped such that the rope started on a small diameter to give maximum lifting force and subsequently moved onto a larger diameter as the engine accelerated up to speed. However, this arrangement resulted in the cage at the pit bank being on the large diameter whilst that at the pit bottom was on the smaller diameter. Thus for one turn of the drum the cages would move a different distance.

As the cages had three decks to load and unload special arrangements were needed to accomplish this efficiently. The usual method was to build a level for each deck to allow simultaneous loading for the same position of the winding engine. However at Astley Green the problem was solved in an interesting manner.

At the pit bottom inset, a pair of hydraulic platforms were arranged, connected by a valve under the control of the onsetter at that point. When the cage arrived at pit bottom, it was landed carefully on the table so that the lowest deck was level with the inset. The engineman then wound off extra rope sufficient for the total movement which would be needed. He was then free to carry out his own decking operations in conjunction with the banksman at the pithead.

Meanwhile, at the pit bottom, the tubs or men were exchanged on the bottom deck, and then, under the control of the onsetter, the platform was lowered to bring the second deck of the cage into line, at the same time raising the empty platform by an equivalent amount. That deck was changed and the whole operation repeated for the top deck. By this time the decking operations at pit head would also be concluded and when all was ready, the engineman could gradually take up the slack and wind normally.

The heights of the three decks were unequal, the top deck being the most commodious at 6ft.6in high, while the lowest was only 4ft.6in high. Men today still remember the uncertain feeling of descending in the cramped confines of the lower deck into the bottom of the shaft while the two upper decks were filled above their heads.

A report indicates that the cages in No.1 shaft were not arranged symmetrically in the shaft so that a third cage could be added to work independently of the other two (presumably using the existing capstan engine or a replacement in the same location). There is no record of this having been done. However, as a consequence of this arrangement the west cage was very close to the shaft brickwork and was liable to rub in places.

Screens
Output from the pit needed to have any dirt and rock removed and then the coal needed segregating by size. The initial screening plant was only a temporary affair, and the coal transport system reflected it. Coal from No.2 shaft was landed directly at the screens, while that from No.1 had to be hauled down to No.2 and the empties back again. This soon came to an end when the permanent screens were constructed by Messrs. Heenan and Froude between the pitbank and the canal, roughly half way between the two shafts.

A view of the Astley railway sidings. In the background can be seen the two headgears (No 2 still has the temporary headgear), the winding houses and the original screens (with the oval shaped roof).

The old screens – with the foundations of the new screens in the foreground

The "new" screens under construction c1915

View of the new screens from the canal circa 1920

Belt drives in the new screens.

The new screens c1915

The screen house was of steel girder construction, built over the railway tracks to simplify loading. It was designed to handle 3,000 tons of coal a day. The tubs were raised to the tipping level by creepers from both pit heads. They then ran by gravity through the house to the tippers, executed a U turn and then returned under their original entrance to a second set of creepers which returned then to their respective pit heads.

Initially there were 7 picking belts and appropriate screens. The whole arrangement was electrically driven by no less than 21 motors of various sizes. The plant was extended in 1915, eventually bringing the capacity to 300 tons per hour. The screens were worked by women (known locally as "Pit Brow Lasses") and also by men who due to health reasons were not able to work underground.

Boilers

The steam boiler plant was between and to the north of the two winding houses, and had considerably expanded with the development of the colliery. It consisted, by 1919, of some 13 Lancashire type boilers, each 30 ft. long and 8 ft. in diameter. Only the firing floor was covered in, with corrugated iron, the boilers themselves only being protected by brickwork, the main steam ranges being exposed above them.

The flue gases passed through banks of Greens' Economisers and then up the chimneys, these were equipped with induced draft fans at the base and were 6ft.6in. in diameter inside, one reaching 156 ft. into the sky, the other 154 ft. Originally all the boilers were hand fired. Boiler feedwater was obtained from the canal and chemicals were added for softening.

Underground Development

Development of the Trencherbone and Crombouke seams was well established by 1913, but things did not go as planned. When the Lion's Bridge faulting came to be proven, it was found to have a throw of only 70 feet, about half what had been anticipated to enable the Rams coal to be worked from the Trencherbone inset level.

It was decided to continue to work the Rams coal from the No.2 shaft but to regain the seam beyond the fault (now 70ft. below) SE and SW tunnels were driven at a gradient of 1 in 3 and at an angle to the dip of the seam. These tunnels known as "slants" were driven in the 1920s. This involved bringing up the whole of the output from the area up the slants and winding it in No.2 shaft instead of No.1. This caused delays due to working the tubs through the airlocks. The slants were worked by endless over-rope haulage, the tubs being lashed onto the moving haulage rope by chains.

Hospital Fund

The Minute Book from the meetings of the Hospital Fund has survived from which the following has been extracted.

The fund was started on 23rd December 1918 and contributions from the workforce was 1d per week. This was increased to 2d in 1938, 3d in 1942, and finally to 4d in 1946. The first hospitals to receive funds were Leigh Infirmary, Salford Royal, Manchester Eye Hospital, and convalescent homes in Buxton and Southport. In 1942 the fund joined a scheme run by Leigh Infirmary who distributed the funds to other hospitals.

The meetings of the Hospital Fund Committee were generally chaired by the colliery manager who signed the minutes along with the Secretary. In its 30 year existence the only Secretary had been Frank Grundy whose neat hand writing fills the record book. He was given a present of £25 when the fund closed on 5th July 1948 for his "long and efficient service to the Hospital Fund". Frank Grundy lived to the age of 90.

Early photo (undated) of No 2 cage. Banksman Joe Kelly is at the left – and he was still doing this job in the 1940's.

Underground conveyor transfer point. 1950's?

THE FORMATION OF MANCHESTER COLLIERIES

By 1928, the Clifton & Kersley Coal Company Ltd. had closed Wet Earth and Spindle Point collieries, Outwood Colliery was being worked by a subsidiary, the Outwood Colliery Co. Ltd., while Newtown had been sold to the Bridgewater Collieries Ltd. who also owned the Sandhole, Mosley Common and Ellesmere collieries.

In the following year, Atherton Collieries Ltd. (Fletcher-Burrows), Bridgewater Collieries Ltd., Speakmans, Astley and Tyldesley Collieries Ltd., Andrew Knowles & Sons Ltd., and the Clifton & Kersley Colliery Co. Ltd., together with its subsidiaries, were merged to form Manchester Collieries, the new formed organisation promptly embarking on a plan of both expansion and consolidation.

Railways

In 1930 a new railway line was laid down to link the colliery with the Bridgewater Collieries line at Boothsbank Tip, about 3/4 of a mile to the east of the pit. This linked Astley into the main colliery railway network and also gave it access to the workshops at Walkden Yard.

The most immediate effect of the new line was to close down the tippler at Astley, on the site of the old tramroad tippler, as the basin at Boothsbank was much larger and allowed the boats to turn. (Draining of the basin in 1991 exposed many Manchester Collieries barges sunk beneath later examples.)

Coal Preparation

The following year a coal washing plant of 150 tons per hour capacity (some records say 120 tons per hour) was erected by Nortons Tividale some distance to the east of the main colliery buildings on the site of Greens Tip and Lodge. Water for the washery was obtained from Whitehead Hall Brook which was described in 1944 as "an insalubrious supply which is the subject of complaint due to the high proportion of sewage".

A dust extracting plant of the Norton Collins type was installed at the main screens, principally to handle the Trencherbone Slack. At around the same time, a Rexman pulverising plant was constructed between the pit bank and the boilerhouse, to deal with the waste coal. The dust extracted from the screens was added to the output from the pulveriser, and this was fed to some of the boilers which were fitted with air blowers to burn it.

The boilers fired on pulverised fuel were the six nearest No.2 Engine House. A somewhat hair raising fire-lighting technique was used on these "dust fired" boilers. This seems to have involved pouring paraffin down a tube into the boiler onto burning paper and then turning the air on which blew the pulverised coal into the boiler firegrate. Sometimes it ignited with a bang! Initial draught was controlled by the insertion of a finger into a small hole in the fire door!

Power

The expansion of the workings brought about by the Rams slant development had vastly increased the compressed air demand and to cope with this, two additional air compressors had been installed. These were erected in the power house and consisted of a mixed pressure turbo-compressor by Fraser & Chalmers and a high pressure turbo-compressor by Hick Hargreaves of Bolton. One at least of these was said to have been transferred from another colliery, possibly Clifton, in 1933.

The electrical output of the colliery had also been augmented by the installation of a 1 Megawatt mixed-pressure turbine also by Fraser & Chalmers, fitted with a Lancashire Dynamo Co. alternator. The distribution system was altered and a substation built to enable power to be bought in from the Lancashire Electric Power Co. if needed.

In 1933 an overhead power line was erected between Astley and the Kirmishaw Nook pit power house, to the north west, it is thought that this was primarily due to problems with the Astley 1 MW alternator in that summer, the new line allowing either pit to supply the other if occasion demanded. Nook also supplied the bulk of the electricity requirements of another Manchester Collieries pit,

Bedford nearer Leigh, and the more adjacent Gin Pit. Manchester Collieries Company policy was to reduce the amount of compressed air used in its pits, as the transmission of electricity was much more efficient. As a result of this, a larger turbo-alternator of 2 MW capacity was installed in the power house at Astley, manufactured by Metropolitan Vickers and G.E.C.

Pit-head Baths

A comprehensive pithead baths, canteen and medical centre was designed for the Miners' Welfare Committee by architect C.Kemp A.R.I.B.A., and constructed in 1935-36 at a cost of over £24,000. The site chosen was at the entrance to the colliery yard, by the side of the road through Higher Green. The layout followed the then most modern practice. Shower bath cubicles, heated lockers for clean and pit clothes were provided to accommodate 2000 workmen.

Baths & canteen as seen from the gate. 1935.

The building, with the exception of the officials' baths, was paid for entirely by the Miners' Welfare Fund. The men were to subscribe 3d. per week towards the cost of running and maintaining the baths, the Company subscribing an equal amount. To mark the opening of the baths the Company presented each user during the first week with a bathing slip, towel and soap.

Ventilation

The make of firedamp (methane) in the colliery was found to be very high, especially when first entering virgin areas and ventilation often became a problem unfortunately with fatal consequences.

An extensive alteration of the underground ventilation system was begun in 1936, bringing the fan delivery to 273,140 cubic feet per minute at 6.7ins. water gauge, one third of which was stated to be reaching the coal faces. This necessitated heavy work throughout the colliery and seriously affected the productivity for 1938/39 and for several years afterwards. However, by that time, large scale developments, described later, absorbed the man-power which had been engaged on the repairs and short term maintenance. Development too, was by 1939 becoming a pressing problem, but 1939 brought something far worse than expenditure...

View from the top of No 1 headgear looking over the lodge behind which was built the new baths and canteen – now the greened area on the left hand side whilst approaching the main gates of the colliery.

THE 1939 DISASTER

The news was announced to the local populace by the News Chronicle for Wednesday, June 7th. The headlines read: *FIVE MEN DIE, FOUR INJURED, IN PIT FIRE EXPLOSION. OFFICIAL, HURT HIMSELF, SAVED FAINTING MAN.* The story was given as follows:

Five men were killed and four injured in a series of explosions while fighting a gob fire in the Crombouke Mine of the Astley Green Pit this afternoon. Tonight, with the bodies of the men, officials and trained fire fighters - still unrecovered, it was decided to seal off the affected part of the pit to prevent further loss of life.

The manager of the pit, Mr. J.H.Hewitt, was killed while leading the fire-fighters, his under-manager, Mr. W.Middleton was seriously injured. Manchester Collieries, Limited, owners of the pit, tonight issued the following statement: "Manchester Collieries deeply regret to report that following a series of slight explosions in the Crombouke Mine at their Astley Green Colliery, five men have lost their lives.

J.H.Hewitt, Manager of the Pit, Allenby Street, Atherton.
G.Griffiths, Under-looker, of Coach Road, Astley.
J.Keegan, fireman, of Henry Street, Tyldesley.
Eli Smith, collier, of Tyldesley Road, Atherton.
William Warhurst, collier, of Second Avenue, Astley.

Four other men have been got out of the mine injured, only one seriously.

Following a conference with His Majesty's Inspector of Mines and the Miners Agent, it was decided to prevent possible further loss of life, to seal off the district affected.

The injured men are:
W.Middleton, of Henfold Road, Tyldesley, Under-Manager.
John Laughton, Under-looker, of Leigh.
Frank Morris, of Lime Street, Tyldesley.
William Smith, of Manchester Road, Astley.

A gob fire was first reported at 12.30 a.m. today, and the night shift of 1000 men was withdrawn from the pit face. Forty men, officials and trained fire fighters were left to fight the fire. They made such progress that by 4 a.m. it was possible for the morning shift to descend. Between 4 a.m. and 6 a.m. 1000 men went down the shaft to the various mines which make up the Astley Pit.

During the morning men were withdrawn from certain sections, and a party of officials, including the men killed and injured, descended. They were working in C panel of the Crombouke Mine, where the gob fire had occurred earlier in the day. Men continued to work in the Rams mine on a lower level, and at 1.30 p.m. news of an explosion reached them. John Skise (25), a collier, of Manchester Road, Tyldesley, told me that he was working in the Rams mine. "I didn't hear any explosion, but there is such a racket that it would have to be tremendous for us to hear it in our seam. A fireman came and said: "There's trouble in the Crombouke mine. There are men there. I want you lads to come and help me get them out." "When I got there it was very hot and there was smoke hanging about.

I helped to carry Mr. Middleton out. He seemed to be very badly injured. He had got out Frank Morris, one of the other men. Although he was hurt himself, he had dragged Morris, who was fainting for 200 yards. At one stage he stopped to release air from a pipe into Morris' face to revive him. They told me that Bill Smith was further along, but the fireman said there was too much gas to go after him.

Three chaps said they'd have a go and came back with Bill Smith. They were George Marger, William Hulme and Richard Sutton. I think Mr. Middleton's effort was the bravest thing a man could do. He was in no state to walk himself, let alone help others." Another rescue workman told me that the 40 men left to fight the fire used sand and a tank holding 199 gallons of water. "Those men are heroes" he said.

Following the explosion a call was sent to the mines rescue Station at Boothstown and men equipped with every device for fighting the fire were hurried to the scene. Ten rescue men, who had been putting on their breathing equipment as they were being driven to the pit immediately went down. They were met by other explosions before they had time to reach the five men now given up as lost.

The Astley Green Pit is one of the most modern in the Lancashire Coalfield, and is at present employing 2000 men. It was sunk in 1908 and this is the first serious accident there has been. Mr. Hewitt was promoted from Under-Manager about two years ago. His father retired some time ago from the position as Manager at another coal pit. Mr. Hewitt leaves a widow and two sons. The father of Eli Smith, one of the dead men, was killed in the same pit in 1920. Eli Smith was married with one child. His brother, Harry, is also employed in the pit.

There was a notable absence of women waiting at the pit head; at one time not a woman was to be seen among the crowd. I understand that Manchester Collieries immediately informed the relatives of every man who had not escaped unharmed. This prevented the pitiful scenes so frequently a feature of colliery accidents. Tonight lorry loads of bricks and sand are being rushed to the mine.

On the busy East Lancashire Road, a few hundred yards away, a police officer was on traffic duty to facilitate their quick arrival. The bricks and sand are being sent down in the cage for strengthening the barrier which has been built to prevent the fire from spreading. Men who arrived at the colliery to prepare for work the afternoon saw a notice chalked roughly on the wall. It read "No afternoon shift today." Tonight several hundred sightseers gathered in the roadway near the pit head. Few of them were relatives.

One of the injured men Frank Morris has given the following account:

Frank Morris was 34 at the time and was employed as a pan shifter (moving the face conveyor as the coal face advanced). He was working with 3 other men engaged in improving the ventilation into an area of the mine when there was an explosion and "everything went black with coal dust".

Frank became separated from his mates and started to try and find his way out to the shaft. He eventually recognised an area which was in the Rams mine below the Crombouke where he met some other miners who wanted him to wait for a stretcher. However, Frank had only one thought at that time which was "to get out" and he made his way to the shaft. He was taken to Leigh Infirmary suffering from burns and shock.

His wife, hearing about the accident and that Frank was at Leigh Infirmary, immediately caught a tram from Tyldesley to the hospital. During the journey she was told by someone that Frank had died underground, by another that he had died on the pit bank, and yet another told her he thought he had died in hospital.

One can imagine the state this poor lady was in by the time she eventually arrived at the hospital only to be denied any information by the hospital staff who thought that she was a newspaper reporter! Eventually, she was allowed to see her husband for just 5 minutes. He was very much alive although seriously injured. He could not give her a coherent story and "he seemed to be worrying about the fate of the other men down the pit".

It took Frank 6 months to recover which included some time at the Southport convalescent home. He vowed never to go down the pit again and eventually received £250 compensation. The settlement had taken a long time to be paid and it came just in time as the family were down to their last pound and "things were looking very grim". However, Frank insisted that the money was put into savings and he was able to find work, but he never went down the pit again.

The Inquest into the deaths took place in late July, when the Jury returned a verdict of "death from misadventure". The bravery of the men was remarked on by the Coroner. Additional information concerning the disaster was given by Edward Humphrey Browne, the Mining Agent. He said that Hewitt, the dead Manager, had rung him up to say that in the early hours of June 6th. a shot had been fired and some smoke had been seen at another place.

Hewitt was satisfied at the time that the smoke was fumes from the shot. However, after a subsequent message, Browne put into effect the emergency organisation. Twice he spoke to Hewitt over the telephone, but he was emphatic that he could find no trace of the fire. Browne was about to go underground himself to see when a final message was received, "It has gone off again. It has blown us off our feet." Two men volunteered to go down with him.

It was very dusty and difficult to see when they reached the Crombouke delivery level. The safety lamps were burning, albeit low, and the canary was still alive. When they reached the haulage engine, Browne's lamp went out and when another was passed forward the canary appeared to be dead. The party were unable to go further and returned to summon the rescue teams.

The first team were instructed to look for the missing men, but just before they reached the coal face there was a fall and they were stopped. They had passed three bodies on the way and offered to go and get them out. They were told not to, and a second fresh team was sent in instead to see if there was any trace of fire. Browne remained with the stand-by team, and then short circuited the fresh air into the return, to starve any fire of oxygen. He was certain that had the first team been allowed to return then they too would have been lost.

William Granby, the Under-Manager, said that when he went down the mine after the accident there had been a temporary lull in the ventilation and then a sudden reversal of the current. This was the usual sign of an explosion.

It is interesting to note that there appears to be no report from the Inspector of Mines for the 1939 explosion. Such a report is only required if there is a public enquiry which there was not in this case. The colliery would have records but there is no trace of those now. The only records remaining are newspaper reports and the memories of the lucky survivors of whom Frank Morris may be the last.

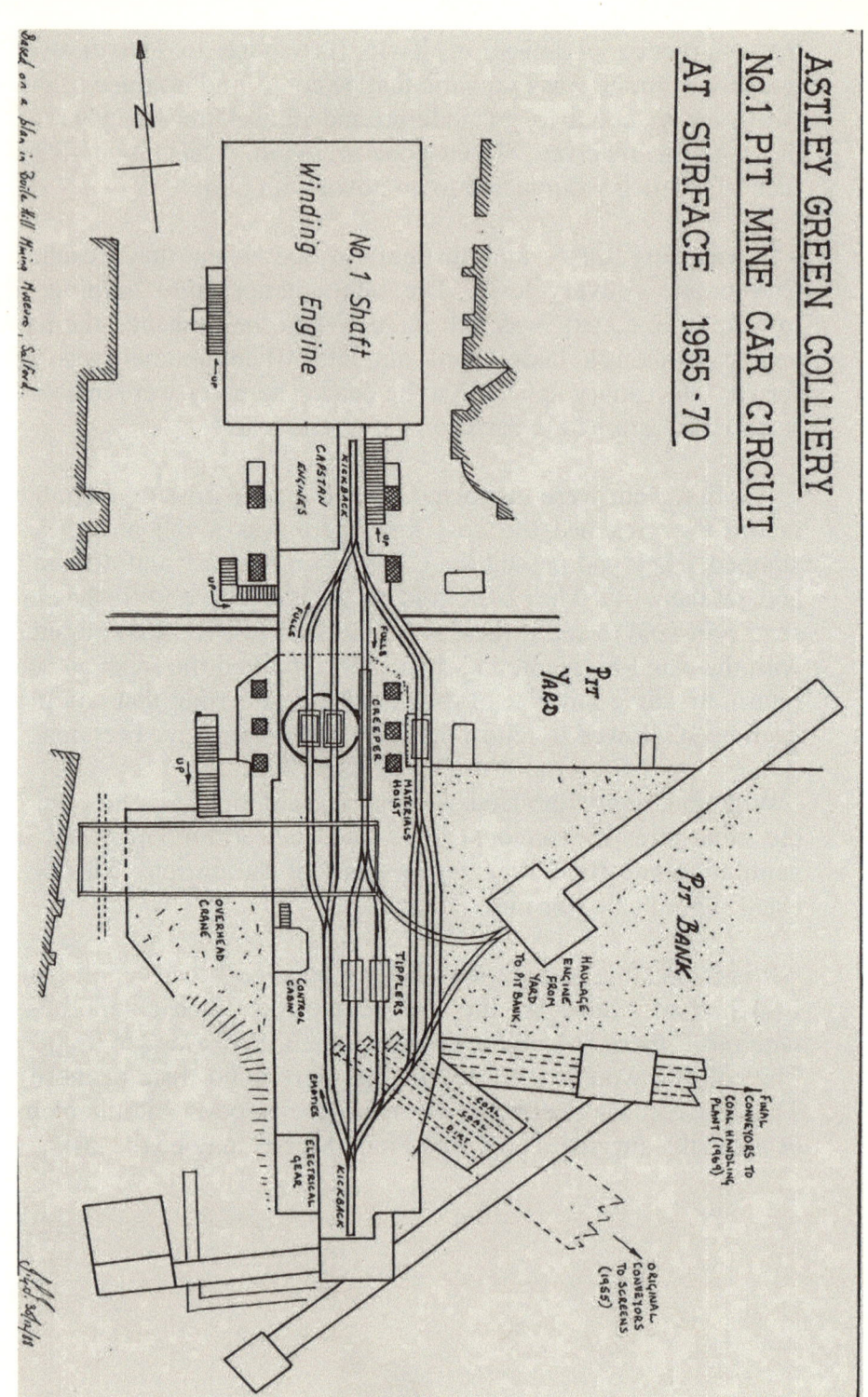

Underground Photo's.

View to the surface of a pit shaft showing the tubbing.

The loco "garage" with a coal hauling engine. Photo is believed to be in the Worsley 4 ft workings.

Locomotive underground.

Coal tippler in the Worsley 4 ft workings

Worsley 4 ft pit bottom with creeper on the right & travelling steps on the left. This led to "West Dips", a working area which did not last long.

Electric winder at Worsley 4 ft installed to wind to pit bottom after No 2 converted to skip winding in 1948.

Turbine pump in Worsley 4 ft.

Haulage engine in Worsley 4ft.

No 1 pit bottom 1950's

No 1 Pit bottom during the change, 1950's

No 1 pit bottom with tubs in the cage. 1950's

Underground tub loading point with small tubs, 1950's

Driving underground heading. Eimco loader. 1950's?

Gablock station.

THE OLD DAYS

Visitors are always welcome at Astley, and it is all the more rewarding when they have something to tell us about "the old days" when Astley was a working pit. Unfortunately, with the passing of time memories get hazier, and they need to be put down before they fade altogether.

We have been very grateful, therefore, to some of our visitors who have taken the time to chat and allow some of their memories to be written down for posterity. Given time, always at a premium, we hope to be able to do more of this work, as important, in its own way, as the restoration of the No.1 Engine itself.

A Rope Change with a difference

To give an idea of the scale of problems involved in mining, mostly hidden from the public eye, and lost forever when a mine is closed, the following description is worth recounting. The South-West slant was an over-rope haulage driven by a 150 h.p. electric winding plant. This hauled 10 cwt. tubs a distance of up to 1540 yards up a varying gradient, the steepest section being 400 yards of 1 in 3, only 120 yards being level at the bank head. The seam gradient was 1 in 6 in the direction of the slant, but the presence of faults led to several severe changes of gradient in the actual trackbed.

The winding rope was 3,400 yards long, 1.25ins. in diameter and was of the Lang's Lay flattened steel wire rope type, manufactured from best plough wire with a breaking strain of 65 tons. The slant, in the early 1940's, was hauling about 500 tons of coal per shift on a 6 shift per week basis, plus a certain amount of dirt from repairs and development work.

The tubs of 15 cwt. capacity were attached to the rope by wrought iron lashing chains of 0.5ins diameter and 12 feet long. The tubs were arranged in gangs of two full tubs when ascending and four empty tubs when descending. The slant delivered the tubs to the No.2 (upcast) shaft, via an airlock, at the Rams inset, this being approximately 1900 feet from the surface. This was the main winding point in the No.2 shaft.

The No.1 (downcast) shaft inset was at a depth of 1670 feet below the surface, and from this inset a main intake roadway had been driven on the full dip (i.e. at 1 in 4) and connected with the slant at a point about 50 yards inbye of the slant hauler. A new rope had been installed at Easter 1939, but this was badly worn at a splice joint and a new one was required. This old rope had been installed in a single length with only one splice, due to the heavy duty required and it was intended to fit the new one in a similar manner. However, the original installation had been done by lowering the rope down the No.2 shaft with the No.2 capstan engine. The end had been spliced to the old rope and then wound round by the hauler, the old rope being cut off in short lengths, coiled and then sent up later. This had taken 30 hours of difficult and arduous work.

This could not be afforded under wartime circumstances and somehow the task of rope changing had to be completed in the time available - Saturday afternoon and Sunday without interfering with the normal winding arrangements for the weekend shifts. In the event, a complex operation was evolved and carried out with the No.1 capstan engine lowering the new rope down No.1 shaft.

This was diverted at the Rams inset and joined on to the end of the old rope after that had been cut. The No.2 capstan engine lowered a cable to the Rams inset in that shaft which was attached to the other end of the haulage rope. Then, as the No.2 capstan engine hauled up the old rope, the No.1 capstan engine paid out the new one until it was in place. All that required doing then was the splicing. Work had begun on the lowering operation at 12.30 p.m. on the Saturday and was completed by 10 p.m. the same day.

The rope was spliced on the Sunday morning, the length of the splice being some 120 feet - 10 yards for every inch of circumference. The time taken was no less than 5 hours. During the following week the stretch of the new rope was taken up, this being about 12 yards. The whole operation was one of the last operations of this type at Astley, as the development of the tunnels described later removed the need for the slant haulages, and the No.2 shaft was put to other uses.

The Winding Rope Changing Procedure

The following account of the rope changing procedure has kindly been provided by **"Jimmy" Jones**, for many years the surface foreman at Astley Green and well known dialect poet of Tyldesley.

"The cage was first brought up to the top deck level. A flat cart was run in and wedged, carrying two large sectioned girders which were to carry the weight of the cage when lowered. Then two strong railway sleepers were laid across the outside edges of the shaft. The cage was then lowered so that the girders rested on the sleepers. Four square wooden chocks were then placed to on the girders to receive the cage rim. The cage chains and detaching hook were then lowered slowly onto the stationary cage top and the rope capel unbolted and drawn out onto the pit bank.

"After being wrapped with holding wire in two places, the rope was burned through between them. The loose end was then pulled from the pit bank by a mobile crane to a large steel drum mounted on a railway bogey and attached to it. The old rope was then wound on to the drum by a combination of the main winding engine lowering the rope and the drum being driven through gearing by a compressed air engine."

"When the rope had unwound from the main winding drum to the point where it passed through the bull hole on to the inner spool, the job was stopped while a capstan rope was clamped onto the winding rope. The inner spool was then unbolted, the safety clamps taken off, and the tail end brought out and made fast onto the receiving drum. The old rope on its drum was then moved away and the new rope moved into position. This was mounted on another bogey with simply a shaft to turn on. Its speed of pay off was governed by men holding planks which acted as brakes on the drum rims, and by making the winding pulley over which it passed rigid."

"The new rope was led back by the same procedure up to the bull hole where it was attached to the inner spool. The inner spool was attached by gearing to a small compressed air engine which was fastened down for the purpose next to the main winding drum in the engine house. The head blacksmith then measured off 90 yards which was wound onto the inner spool. This was then re- bolted to the main drum and the compressed air engine disengaged. Six large clamps at alternate angles were then tightened onto the rope behind the bull hole, and the main winding engine then took over to wind the rest of the rope onto the main drum."

"Once the whole rope had been wound off the supply drum, the head blacksmith then bound and burnt off any excess over the usual length of 1050 yards. The loose end was then slowly eased onto the pit bank, laid on trestles and the capping block slid on. This was wrapped by pliable wire about 18 inches from the end. The individual wires in the loose end of the locked coil rope were then splayed out into a conical shape in preparation for capping.

"The capel was drawn forward to encase the splayed wires, and the whole assembly lifted into a vertical position. The capel was then heated up by a large burner to receive 75 lbs of molten white metal, which was poured in from the top. This was then left to cool for about two hours with a jet of compressed air playing on it until it was completely set."

"Finally the rope would be drawn forward to recouple it to the detaching hook and cage chains. The wedges and girders would be withdrawn and the engine man would then run the cages through the shaft, bringing the newly roped cage to the bank to get his deck marks on the drum correct. Sometimes adjusting blocks would have to be put in between the detaching hook and the cage chains to get this just right. This involved repeated sessions of movements with the girders in place and then removed again for each adjustment.

Usually after a further weeks winding further adjustments would have to be made to allow for the rope stretch. The rope was re-capped every six months, a six foot long section being cut off and sent to Walkden Yard for examination and testing of its breaking strain, which was about 150 tons."

Kenneth Terry was an apprentice and then fitter for a time at the age of 18 and remembers some of the men he worked with around 1946 before he left for the Merchant Navy. Ken remembers well the occasion he stood over a loop of cable on the little incline up to the No.1 pitbank. This was worked by a small haulage engine under cover at the top. He got a "clout" behind his ear and hurriedly moved - he didn't know what for until the bloke working the engine showed him his artificial foot - he had done exactly the same thing when he was a lad, but the engine had started and the tightening cable had cut his foot off.

The Foreman Blacksmith was Harry Burton who lived behind the coalyard. He built all the trackwork and crossings etc., at the foot of the shaft and on the surface for the new mine car circuit at No.1 Shaft. The Foreman Fitter at the time was Percy Hope, who lived at the back of Maddison Avenue(?). Jacob Latham, who lived just past the bridge over the canal was the Engineer and Enginewright.

On the No.2 Shaft, the door of the skip used to stick partly open and would jam in the shaft, so anyone working in No.2 had to walk round to No.1 to come up.

Raising the No 1 pulley wheel, c1911

More Underground photo's

Untidy underground tunnel with conveyor on right.

Manoeuvring tubs underground.

Underground tunnel with conveyor and "fire service" tank wagon.

End of an underground tunnel possibly showing the face.

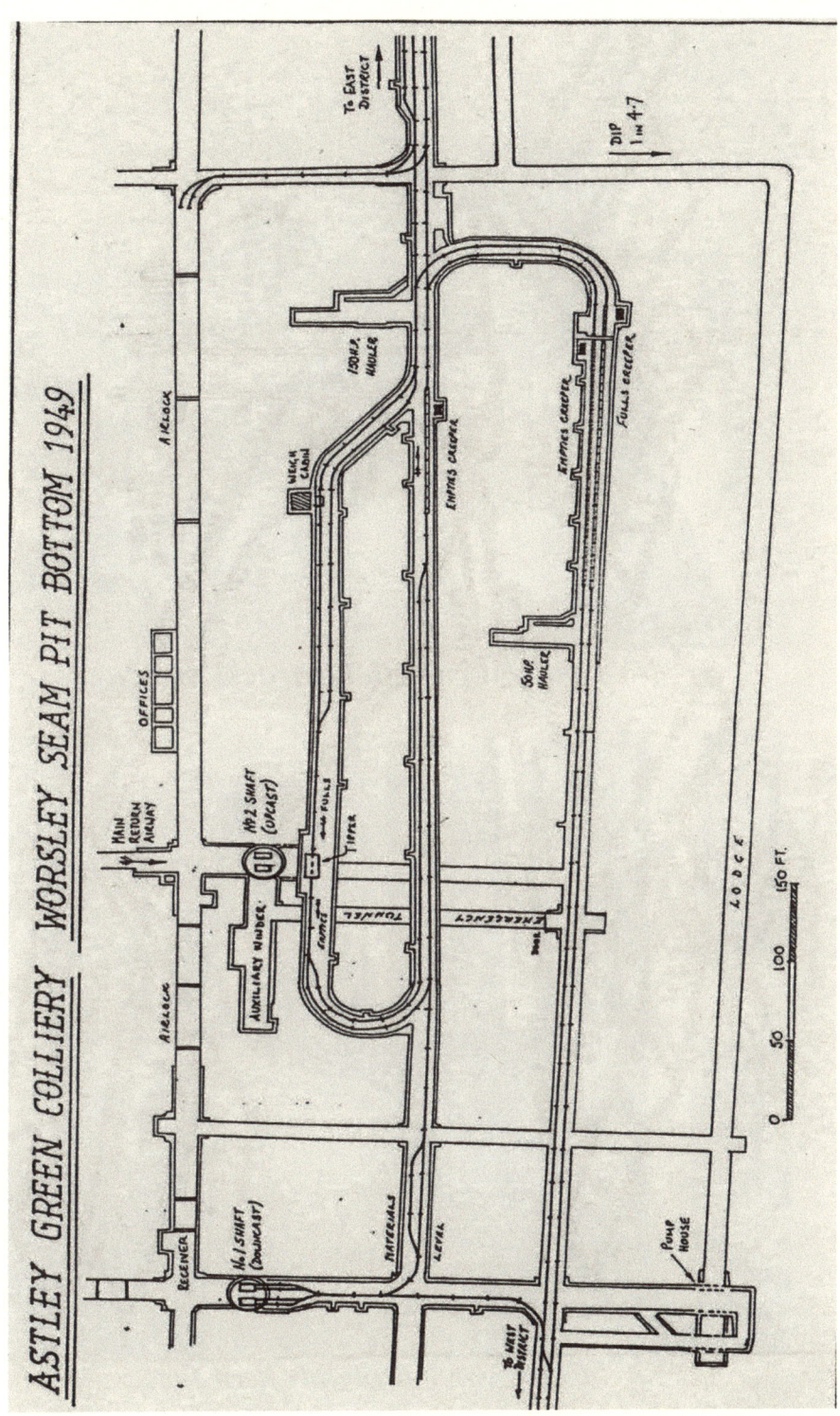

No 1 pit bottom with tub tracks and cage.

Conveyor – probably near face.

NEW DEVELOPMENTS

Astley was relatively little troubled by the war, although one engineer remembered the problems of carrying a red hot metal yoke for the winding engine across to the engine house from the forge at dead of night, the yoke glowing for all to see! In August 1940, several bombs fell to the south of the Colliery, but it was not until long afterward that it was discovered that they had, indeed, been aimed at the pit.

The Company was shown a German map which indicated the colliery by a red outline and which was headed accordingly. Air raid shelters were constructed at the south of the site. They were incorporated into the bank for the headshunt for the railway serving the screens.

Rams, Binn, Crombouke, and Trencherbone Seams

The Rams was reported in 1944 to be "the best mine available". It had a top section to the coal called the "Penny" which was left where possible to secure the strata above. Conversely, the Trencherbone mine which was good household coal with a low ash content had serious roof problems. Convergence was noticed at the face between the beginning and end of the shift - "nothing is ever still in this mine". As a consequence the seam was considered to be making a loss at that time.

In 1940 the Rams seam reached by the slants was becoming worked out above the slants and the seam was dipping away from the fault. However, the Binn seam was in process of major development. This engendered a considerable re-organisation. A pair of level tunnels was begun in 1941 from the No.1 and No.2 pit bottoms to strike the Binn, Crombouke and Rams seams to the dip on the south side of the fault. The Crombouke had not been worked for 4 years after the 1939 disaster as the colliers were unwilling to enter the mine. However, a new development was also proposed to the north east towards Mosley Common.

Worsley Four Feet Seam

Simultaneously with the above scheme, it was decided to use the No.2 shaft to develop the Worsley Four Foot seam, which had hitherto remained untouched, as it was both heavily watered and also worked by the older collieries to the north, their workings extending to about 110 yards to the north of the Astley shafts.

An experimental room-and-pillar working was begun to the east in 1944, in which seepage of water from the old workings proved troublesome, so much so that the main intake and return roadways had to be flanked by a parallel drainage road to the dip side. After a period of trial, the main roads were carried forward in the solid ground to a point where the old workings began to curve away towards the north, when a further experimental working was opened out. Thereafter conditions became progressively easier and after the limit of the old workings was reached, it was possible to open out a longwall face and begin normal production.

Profiting by this experience a second district was opened out to the west and it was found possible to work this by longwall methods also. Although a number of feeders of water were struck to the dip, these produced a constant make of water so with the provision of suitable pumps, the water could be controlled. Locomotive haulage was not considered at this time because of the problem of levels, especially on the far side of the Chaddock Fault.

Some experimental work was done in the Worsley seam using different explosives. In particular powder was found to be superior to the normal Cardox burster device in the preparation of the coal. In addition in view of the large numbers of "fizzers" - misfires - with Cardox, Astley carried out careful trials with heaters in order to ascertain whether the lower or higher range of electrical resistance being used gave the best results. The trials were inconclusive, but certainly revealed the need for greater care underground and careful selection by the manufacturers.

Accidents

The accident rate within the Manchester Collieries was described as "distressingly high", indeed in 1946 Astley was 11th. in the league table of accidents with only 949 man-shifts per accident. Gibfield Colliery at Atherton was the top of the league with no less than 1533 man-shifts per accident.

Some of the causes were failure to adhere to the support rules for the faces, falls of side dirt or coal, withdrawing of supports and working under the unsupported roof, insecure scaffolding and not taking shelter from shot-firing. An intensive safety propaganda campaign was initiated, loud-speaker broadcasts being given at changes of shift, the first arrangement being tried at Astley. However, as it was thought that the banksmen might be distracted if the broadcasts were made at the pitheads, they were given in the lamproom.

Skip Winding

The Worsley development was a success and as output increased it became necessary to provide suitable pit bottom and winding arrangements to handle it. The No.2 shaft was originally equipped in a similar manner to the No.1 with 3-deck 12-tub cages, however, as No.1 shaft was the downcast and No.2 the upcast, it was desired to maintain the haulage in intake air.

In cage winding, this involved passing the tubs through air locks at the pit bottom and at bank, a labour intensive operation involving no less than 26 men. However, after investigation of other collieries, it was decided to install a skip-winding system in the No.2 shaft to wind purely from the Worsley seam. In this system no working through air-locks would be required, as the skip would remain in the shaft and could be sealed at loading and unloading to suitable bunkers which would act as airlocks. There would also be a considerable saving in man-power, and so, despite the known fragility of the Worsley coal, it was adopted.

The meeting of the No.1 and No.2 Pit workings early in 1946 meant that there would be no problems with the Rams coal, hitherto wound up No.2 shaft, as this could now be diverted to the No.1 shaft via Browne's Tunnel at No.5 South-West Level. The proving in the South-West Rams Mine had confirmed that the last fault encountered was of some 170 yards upthrow to the South. The White and Black seams had also been confirmed in the proving.

Installation of the new pit bottom was carried out without interruption to the existing cage winding system. Over the section due for excavation to form the necessary pocket chambers, half rings of tubbing were let into the shaft wall and all operations carried out behind them. The shaft gear, cages etc. were all modified over the summer holiday of 1947, work beginning on the Friday evening July 4th 1947.

The first coal was drawn by skip on the 23rd. August. During the changeover period, No.1 shaft was placed on a double shift to maintain production. Below the skip loading level, the remainder of the shaft was accessed by a small electric winder - the "emergency winder" it was called, while at the surface, the screening plant was extended to handle the new coal, the new section being constructed by Messrs. W.H.Barker & Sons.

A group of miners with bottle lamps outside the baths at Astley Green colliery. The photo was taken in 1935.

Workmen on No 2 c1916

Coal picking belts

Workmen with the tippler in the new screens.

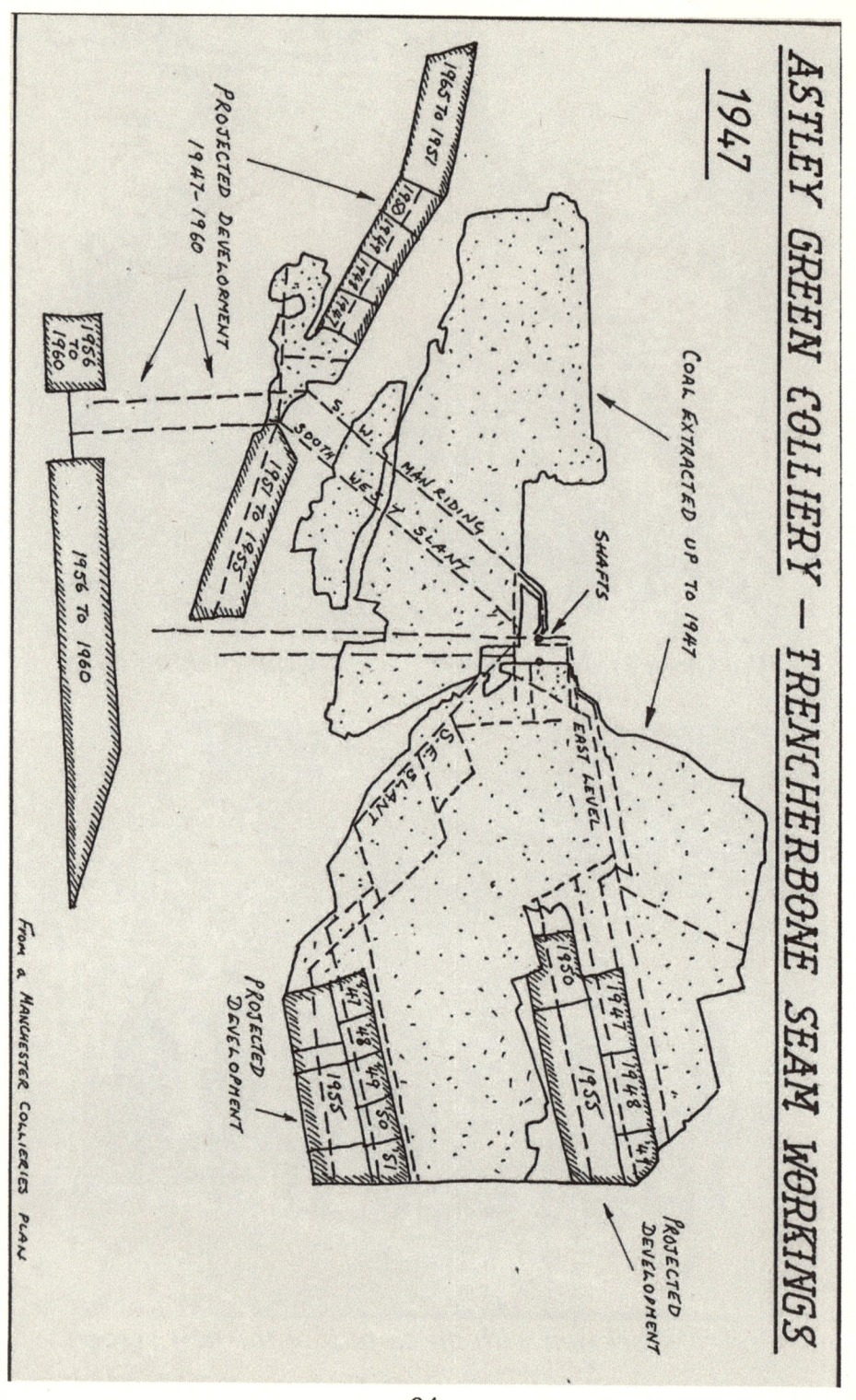

NATIONALISATION AND AFTER

Britain had elected a Labour Government in 1945, and as a result the dreams of the miners' unions became reality. They had been pressing for many years for the public ownership of the collieries and at midnight on the 31st. of December, 1946, the Coal Industry Nationalisation Act became law, and the collieries became public property. Thus 1st January 1947 was "Vesting Day", when the Manchester Collieries Company ceased to be a private concern and became just another district of the National Coal Board.

The news of the forthcoming events had been distributed to the Colliery Officials in the previous February in Issue No.13 of the Manchester Collieries' Newsletter, written by E.H.Browne, the General Manager. At that time the Act was still only a Bill going through the Committee Stage. He said, "The Bill does not, as yet, give any guarantee to staff but it is hoped some change may be made in it..... The Nationalisation of the industry is a step of such major importance that it will call upon the greatest efforts of all concerned to carry over the changes, and as far as officials of this Company are concerned I have no doubt that they will not spare themselves in this respect."

The colliery owners were compensated by national arbitration and by a valuation board. In preparation for this event, the Manchester Collieries had had a comprehensive technical report on their assets compiled by Humphrey Browne, their General Manager, in which details of the colliery plant and development proposals up to the vesting day were clearly laid out.

Astley figured largely in these proposals as one corner of an integrated programme involving Mosley Common, Sandhole and Newtown collieries. This was intended to access the "extensive south coalfield" whose estimated resources were put at over 143 million tons. This excluded doubtful seams and those which had not been worked before. The limit in depth of working was given as 4,500 feet, although this was considered to be a conservative figure. The facilities of the colliery were described as "excellent", an adjective applied to the condition of shafts and also machinery!

In 1946, production had totalled 401,810 tons, these being produced as follows:

Worsley (developing) 16,742
Binn 135,240
Crombouke 29,073
Rams 49,141
Trencherbone 171,614.

The winding capacity was quoted to be of the order of 2,500 tons per week, excluding Saturday and was expected to rise to 3,000 tons by 1952. This was based on single shift winding, and it was remarked that it could be increased at any time, the plant not being fully stretched even then, or by double shift winding.

In the South West Trencherbone haulage an electrical man-riding train had been put into use. In No.1 shaft the transport system was scheduled to be changed from the 10 cwt. tubs to 3 ton-mine cars by 1952, one carried on each deck of the cage. At the heapstead, the old handling arrangements were to be done away with to permit fully mechanised handling of the mine cars.

The actual winding gear and headgear required no modification and the shaft was said to be "admirably suited" to the task. At the pit bottom, mechanical handling was also to be installed as that was to become the principal haulage level, the No.2 shaft being used only for ventilation and emergency egress. Interconnection with the combined Mosley Common, Sandhole and Newtown workings was provided as soon as was convenient at the level of the tunnels and the return horizon at 633 yards depth. The two levels were common to the whole scheme and the workings were intended to be integrated between them.

The haulages in the No.1 pit were intended to be on the Continental principle served by locomotives. Staple shafts were to be sunk connecting the various seam horizons and delivery roads were to be fitted with chutes for lowering coal to the main tunnels and cages for raising men or materials. This was not considered suitable for the friable Worsley coal, where smaller 1 ton tubs and trunk conveyors were to be used.

By the vesting date the two tunnels from the pit bottom, that from No.1 shaft being known as "Richards'" tunnel and that from No.2 being "Browne's" tunnel, had been driven for 2,440 yards to the south, the two tunnels being 16 ft. by 13 feet and 13 feet by 10 feet respectively. In No.1 pit the two main tunnels were extended further to the South through a second upthrow fault of 170 yards to intersect the Crombouke and Rams seams again to the South of the fault. At the same time tunnels were driven to the North of No.1 shaft pit bottom to gain access to the Haigh Yard seam.

Pit Bank

Following the introduction of mine cars in No.1 pit a simpler layout was devised to shuttle the mine cars directly from the cages to two parallel tipplers, the coal being fed to the screens via conveyors. This involved the cars being mechanically propelled from the cage to the tippler running up kick-backs behind the tipplers and then returning to await the empty deck of the next cage. One of the banksmen, Bob Mayo, was badly injured on this arrangement, when he was re-roading a mine car with his back to it when the hydraulic ram operated, knocking him down and breaking his thigh.

V.Keavney says that the cages could hold 30 men per deck. There were sidings on either side of the cages capable of holding three mine cars. The initial direction of movement into and out of the cages was towards the No.1 Engine House, where the full cars were rammed up a kick-back and then ran back round the outside of the shaft past the waiting empties to the single car tipplers. The car contents fell into holding pockets which diverted the material either to the run-of-mine coal conveyor or the dirt conveyor, as appropriate.

From the tippler the empty cars ran up another kick-back before returning towards the cages. There were two separate circuits for the two cages, with a cross-over after the last kick-back to allow for changeovers. On the east side there was a double loop of track which by-passed the tippler and allowed other materials and stores to be run into and out of the cages. This connected with a vertical hoist by the side of the headgear, and via a triangle of track to a short incline between the two headgears. Many men also remember the brazier set burning at the top of the intake shaft to prevent the formation of icicles at the shaft head, and their projectile like descent into the depths. Even so in very cold weather the shaft team had to periodically remove ice from the shaft.

Hydraulic Chocks

Stephen Farrow was a Grade 1 Deputy or Overman from 1957 to 1970, before which he had been a Coal Cutterman. He remembered that on the Worsley 4-East face in the early 1950's they had some of the first Gullick hydraulic chocks, some 246 of them on the one face, worth millions of pounds even then. He was roused from bed one night by the duty man and rushed to the face, to find it collapsed along its whole length, burying the chocks, a Panzer Conveyor and an Anderton Shearer-Loader!

On investigation, the relief valves were found to have failed, allowing the weight of the roof to compress the chocks to their minimum extent. To recover the materials the face had to be dinted and dug out. The chocks themselves could only be removed by firing as they were jammed between roof and floor. The result was that Gullick's fell out of favour with the N.C.B. and were told that until such time as they could guarantee their chocks performance no more orders would be placed with them.

Anderton Shearer-Loader

In the Crombouke No.1 West face, before it was abandoned, the coal was of very good quality, and also free from faults so that cutting could proceed smoothly and efficiently. However there was one cutter who was just too quick and had earned the appellation "Mad" Jolly. Most operators ran the Anderton Shearer-Loader at a gentle walking pace around 10-14 feet per minute - but not Mad Jolly - he ran it on full air and power at around 28 feet per minute stalking along beside it as it tore along the face, coal pouring away from it onto the face conveyors.

Mr. Farrow, on duty at the pit bottom, always knew when Jolly was at work for very soon after the shift began he would receive a frantic call from the man at the Crombouke loading point where the conveyor coal was transferred to the 3-ton mine cars for the journey to the pit-bottom. "You've done it again!" would be the complaint,

"That mad man's at it. Its coming over here like a river!" And so it was, so fast and so thick that the loading point could not cope.

Mr. Farrow remembers timing the loading with his watch. Jolly's coal was coming off the conveyor fast enough to load a 3-ton mine car every forty seconds. Trains consisted of 24 mine cars plus a diesel locomotive. When Jolly was at work the drivers had a busy time, all the pass byes and wagons had to be used to keep things running.

Coal News in February 1963 reported that Astley was approaching an output of 30 cwt per man-shift. This was made possible by the installation of powerful shearer loaders worked on a double shift basis.

Power
Kenneth Terry remembers the layout of the Power House around 1946. In the Power House, from west to east were:

A Bellis & Morcom set.
A Fraser & Chalmers Turbine, driving a generator.
A G.E.C. Turbo-Generator
A Hick Hargreaves Turbo Blower
Possibly another Air Compressor.
The Stairs to the lower floor & Switchboards.
Foundations (Probably used for the compressor for the Armstrong Airbreaker which was installed in the mid 1950's in the powerhouse, this supplied air at 12,000 p.s.i. for coal breaking purposes.)

To the south of the Power House, between it and the bunkers, was the Jackwell, while to the east end of the House was the water softening plant.

Pit Waste
During the early part of 1950, investigations were made into the possibility of introducing pneumatic stowing of waste underground at Astley and it was agreed to carry out a trial on the No.1 East face in the Victoria seam. The face was 255 yards wide with a central loading gate road. The seam was 3ft. 4in. thick with a daily output of some 438 tons.

Pneumatic stowing had not been envisaged when the face had been laid out, but the presence of the central roadway was convenient for the purpose. Excellent progress was made and stowing operations commenced on the 20th. of February, 1950. Only the Worsley seam dirt seemed unsuitable for use, but the rest of the pit dirt was deemed suitable for the job.

At this time, all pit dirt was being collected on the surface on a troughed belt feeding a 20 ton bunker. This was loaded via shaker shutes into lorries for disposal to the dirt fields locally known as the rucks to the south of the canal. Dirt for pneumatic stowing was extracted by placing 2.25in. square mesh in the shutes, the material run off being water sprayed and loaded into tubs for sending underground.

After some trouble with fine dirt the mesh size was increased to 3in. square, but even so an occasional blockage was caused. Boiler ash and rubble were added which reduced the trouble, but eventually the best material was found to be the discard from the washery. The dirt was stocked underground during one winding shift and stowed during the other shift. The tubs were then passed on for use with coal in the normal way. The stowing machine used was of the Markham Blastower type rated at 120 cubic yards per hour.

The final method of dirt disposal, as related by **Jimmy Jones**, for many years the surface foreman, consisted of a fleet of "Internal Use Only" railway wagons. These were filled and shunted to the Astley Moss disposal site and by use of wagon tipplers, shutes and conveyor belts, the waste was carried and spread in layers by a large bulldozer. This operated up to three-quarters of a mile away, the bulldozer pushing dirt away in a radius of approximately 30 yards from the point of delivery on a 25 to 30 foot drop.

Ventilation

The ventilation arrangements were also altered, an electrically driven Walker-Macard adjustable 2-stage axial flow fan, running at 333 r.p.m. was installed, driven by a 1,100 h.p. motor. This was fed by a parallel fan drift to the south of the original one, the steam driven fan was then put on stand-by duty in which it ran noncondensing. However by 1960 the southern extensions of the Rams and Crombouke workings were some 2000 yards or more to the south of the shafts, and it was desired to increase the capacity of the ventilation fan. The Walker-Macard Axial fan was found to be operating close to the theoretical limit and that little improvement in pressure could be obtained from it.

Until a new fan could be built, it was proposed that as a temporary measure the capacity be increased by adding a new axial flow fan in series with the existing one, driven through vee-belts from an 800 h.p. motor. This would, in effect, form a three stage fan providing 620,000 cubic feet per minute at 13.6ins. water gauge. In May, 1960, John Wood & Sons of Wigan were instructed to design and construct the fan structure, installation to take place during the September break. Work on site began during the annual holiday in June, and all was completed to schedule. In the process the old fan house was demolished.

In 1965 this whole system itself became the stand-by fan when a new Sirocco type fan, driven by a 2100 h.p. motor, was installed on the site of and using the old fan drift. This alone was capable of 630,000 c.f.m. and could run at higher outputs if required!

Coal Preparation
The existing screens and separate washing plant were superceded in 1959-60 by a new preparation plant adjacent to the original screens. This was fed directly by conveyor belts from both pit heads and could handle 400 tons per hour.

Boilers
Methane drainage was introduced in the 1950's and while reducing the danger underground, after treatment it was also used on the surface for feeding 5 boilers. Six remained fed by pulverised coal from the screens and pulverising plant while the remaining 5 were fed by Danks' chain gates.

Jimmy Jones recalled that the substantial cost of the Methane drainage scheme to remove the gas from the workings was saved in fuel bills in only 12 months. The range supplied some 2,800 c.f.m. to the boilers at a suction pressure of some 13 inches of Mercury. This itself caused some little difficulty as the flame safety device which was designed to detect an explosive mixture in the range and vent it off kept tripping. Only after extensive testing was it discovered that it was designed to work on a maximum suction pressure or 8 inches, not 13!

In 1961 the existing boiler plant was significantly augmented by a new boiler which was erected to the east of the compressor house. It added a third chimney to the site, but little smoke as the flue gases were passed through an extraction plant. It was constructed by Bennis Combustion Ltd. of Little Hulton and fitted with a stoker by Josef Martin of Munich. It was designed to burn the unsaleable slurry produced by the new screening plant as well as low grade fuel.

The high pressure steam it produced was fed directly to the power house main turbine, and through a reducing valve to the main boiler house steam main. This soon became a cause of trouble as the vast load put upon the steam supply by the two winding engines going on and off load as they wound produced cyclic oscillations in the steam pressure, causing the water tube boiler to be worked inefficiently. One man from the firehole vividly recalls that when the No.1 winder started up, the pressure gauges on the first three Lancashire boilers nearest the engine simply dropped back against their pegs!

The effect of the pressure oscillations in the steam main did not suit the turbine driven alternators and in 1963 the situation was remedied when ten of the Lancashire boilers were modified to act as high pressure steam accumulators on the Daniels (B.B.A.) system two additional low pressure accumulators being added at the same time. The modifications did not affect the availability of the converted boilers for firing, but did much to even out the demand for steam and hence the pressure fluctuations.

FACE SPECIFICATION ASTLEY GREEN COLLIERY WORSLEY W5 FACE

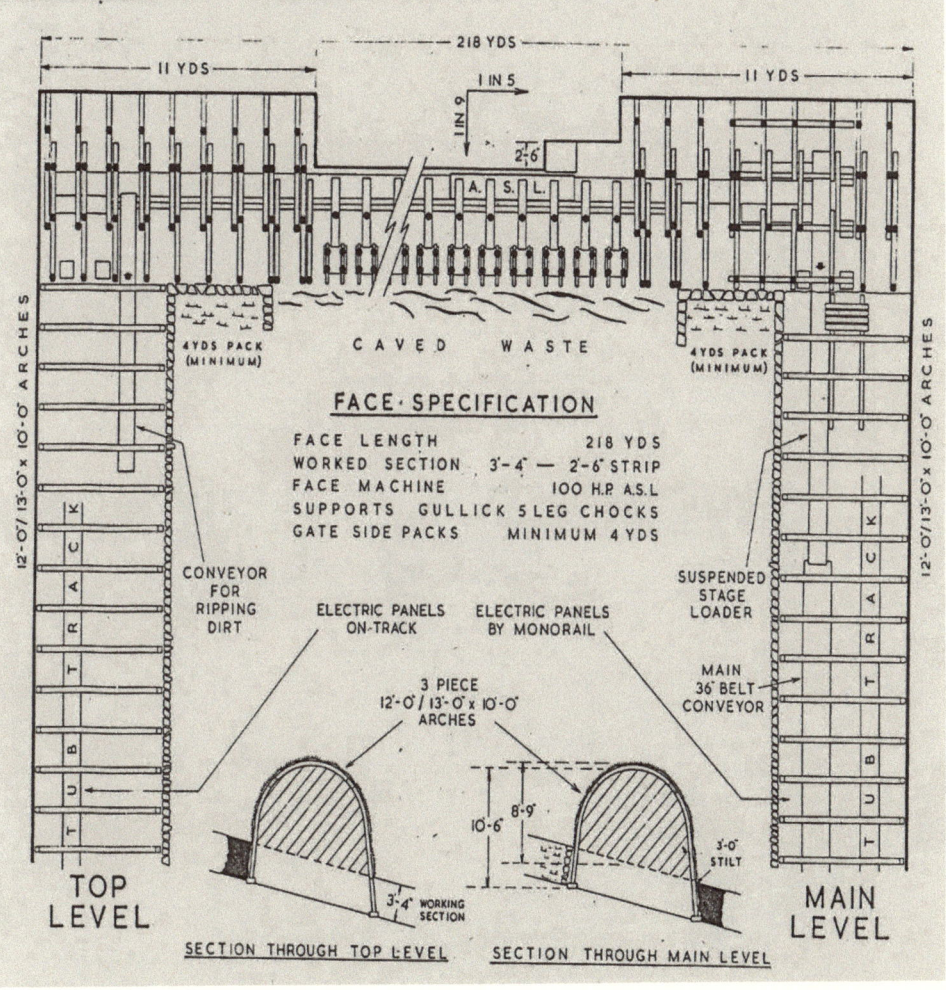

Manpower Deployment Worsley 5's Face.

JOB	First Shift.	Second Shift.	Third Shift.	Fourth Shift.	TOTAL
1. A.S.L. Operators.	1	1		1	3
2. Cablemen.	1	1		1	3
3. Graders.	1	1		1	3
4. Main Gate Stable [includes Boxhole]	5	5		5	15
5. Tail Gate Stable.	4	4		4	12
6. MainGate Ripping.	5	5		5	15
7. Tail Gate Ripping.	4	4		4	12
8. Supports, Abnormalities and Chargehand.	8	8		8	24
9. Stage Loader and Face extension.			6		6
TEAM	29	29	6	29	93
10. Mechanics	1	1		1	3
11. Electricians	1	1		1	3
12. Chock Maintenance	1	1		1	3
13 Face end Deputies	2	2		2	6
TOTAL FACE MANNING	34	34	6	34	108

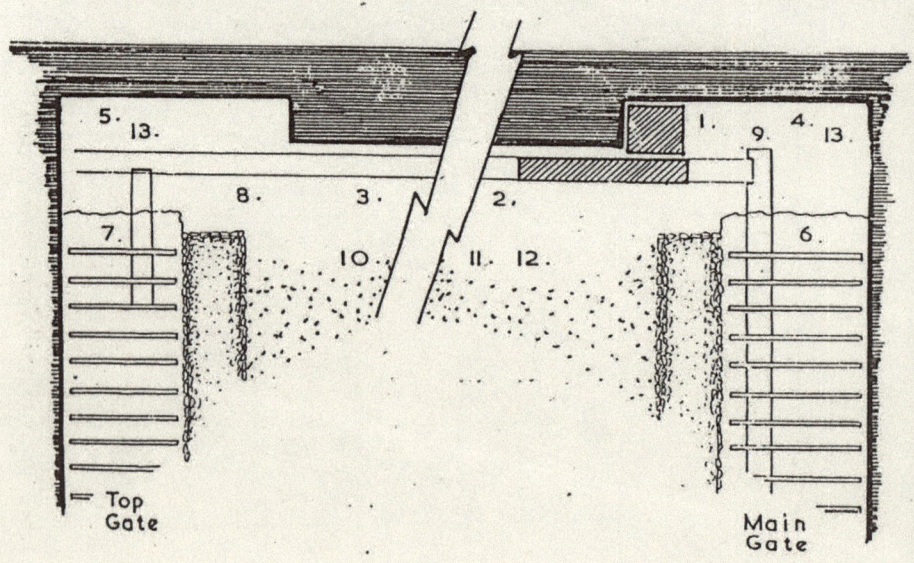

An Astley Green Colliery Pay Tally.

View of the stockyard at the eastern end of the Astley Green site. The photo is taken from the top of the No 2 headgear.

View from the road of Astley Green Colliery taken in the 1930's. On the left inside the gates is the present day museum, the former lodge. No 1 shaft cannot be missed!

No 1 Pit Brow. 1960's

Visit of the Duke of Edinburgh in colliery yard. Visible in picture is J. Wood Manager, F Potter Ch. Wages clerk & H. Hilton in charge of electrical department.

THE 1967 FIRE

In May 1967, an extensive fire occurred in the Crombouke seam. Towards the middle of the day shift on the 18th May a conveyor motor cable was found to be damaged, but as the ripping had been fired, the cable plug was inaccessible, and so the cable was isolated at the main switchgear. Later, while the ripping was being removed by an Eimco electric shovel, its cable was also found to be damaged and was replaced.

Coal shearing began normally with the afternoon shift, but progress was slow where the weak roof had to be closely supported. While the shearer drum segments were being removed in preparation for ploughing the coal onto the conveyor, the shearer was enveloped in large orange flames and sparks which caused minor burns to those nearby. Some of the workmen on the face heard a slight bang and a rush of air, which quickly returned to its usual direction of flow. The air was slightly warmer than usual but with little dust.

It was thought there had been a fall in the waste. However, some other workmen further from the return stable heard a loud bang and immediately saw yellow flames burning in the waste about 15 yards behind the last row of props. The flame was estimated to cover an area 20 yards long. The men raised the alarm and the face was evacuated within a few minutes.

The Eimco operator saw sparks and flames apparently travelling down the trailing cable. A pale blue flame was also seen close to the pack roof. The flame soon appeared at several other places along the 40 yards of ripping and by the time the men had evacuated, the whole 40 yards was ablaze, the trailing cables being consumed by the flames. Two attempts were made to fight the fire. When the district deputy was told that one man had not been accounted for, he took a fire extinguisher and with another man started to walk up the face. After some little distance, they could see that the face was ablaze "from the waste to the coal head" and wisely decided to return. When he arrived back at the main gate he was told that all were, in fact, accounted for.

The second attempt was by a shotfirer, who, with several other men, coupled firehoses up and played water onto the flames. However, as soon as the flames were put out in one place, they reappeared in another. Smoke was increasing all the time and it was decided to leave the district. The men were told to leave the mine as quickly as possible, travelling along the intake airways.

The first news of the fire reached the manager at 3.35 and by 5.55 all men were out of the mine and accounted for. The Senior District Inspector of Mines and NCB Officials were informed and the Mobile Laboratory set up at the mine to monitor the situation. Concern was expressed over the high make of firedamp (methane) in that part of the mine and the possibility that the erection of stoppings to seal off the air would increase the firedamp concentration with the possibility of further and more violent explosions.

After much consideration, two stoppings were erected to control the flow of air through the affected district. These were completed by 5.45 pm on the 19th. May. Monitoring showed little evidence of further explosions, the concentration of methane building up steadily until it passed beyond the explosion range. However, although the concentration of oxygen was soon so low that any fires should be extinguished, concern was expressed that some material would remain hot for some considerable time and that a cooling off period was needed. The evidence suggested a methane ignition had occurred. It was decided to re-open the district in three stages. To begin with the firedamp would be exhausted from the section through the existing methane drainage system. Then controlled leakage of air through the stoppings would begin. Finally the stoppings would be breached, if the first two stages showed favourable conditions.

The first stage of draining the methane was begun at 7.30 am on the 17th. June and by 8.15 am both stoppings were drawing in air. By the 19th June all was ready for the second stage of controlled leaking, but as expert advice thought this would achieve little advantage, plans were made for implementing the third stage.

Work began on the 27th. June at 12.45 pm and by 3.58 pm both stopping plugs had been removed and the doors opened. Continuous monitoring throughout the operation showed no increase in combustion products and it was confidently felt that no active fire remained in the district. The following day progressive and cautious exploration of the district revealed no fires, although the effects of the fire could be seen. This continued until at 8.40 pm on the 29th June, the district was declared safe enough for the work of investigation and restoration to start.

Stephen Farrow also remembers the fire of 1967. One of the men was unaccounted for when the face was cleared, and he and another deputy went in to look for him. It was only after they emerged that they were told he had been found safe at home. He had walked straight past everyone and gone home without saying anything. he was not popular as a result!

A meeting held outside the baths. Photo taken in the 1950's.

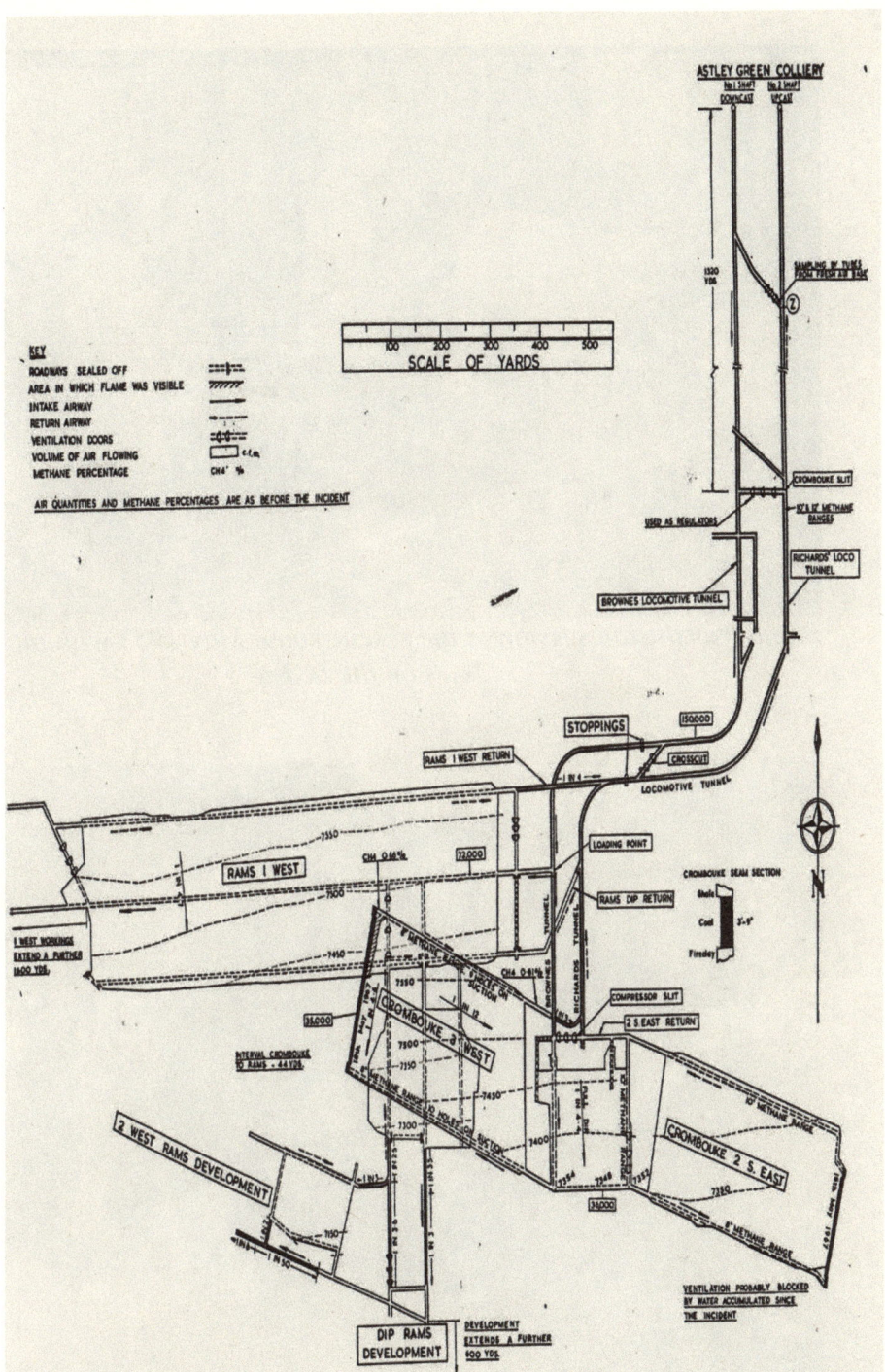

Astley Green Colliery Crombouke Seam, plan of No 3 West Face where an ignition occurred on Thursday 18th May 1967 at 3.25pm

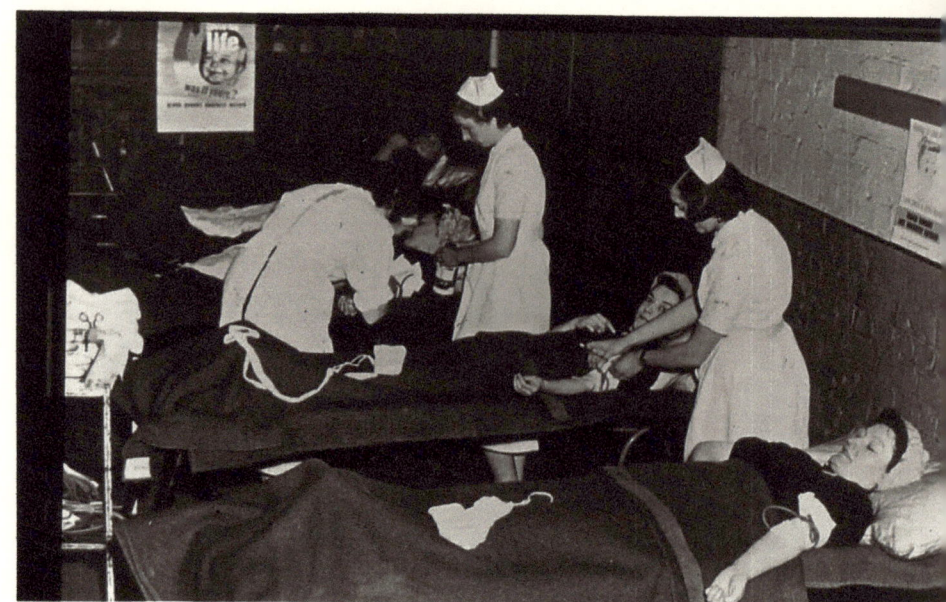
Blood transfusion session in the rescue room May 1953 with pit brow lasses on the beds.

Pit brow lasses at Astley Green. Photo taken around the time of the last war

Pit Brow Lasses on the steps

Pit Brow Lasses at the Christmas Party.

INCREASED OUTPUT

By October 1967 the colliery was producing 2,800 tons of saleable coal per day from 4 faces. These were distributed as follows: one in the Worsley seam, and three in the Yard seam with a standby face in the Crombouke seam as well as development areas in both Crombouke and Rams.

Workable reserves were estimated at over 65 million tons at this time, which at a production rate of 732,000 tons per annum gave over 50 years worth of reserves. **Kenneth Sale** recalls working on the Worsley East face when it was advanced 84ft. 2in. on a 250 yard face in a week - a Lancashire record.

The following two years saw many changes in production faces, the Worsley and Yard seams proving the mainstay. Four faces were worked in the Worsley seam - No.'s 4,5,6 and 7; two in the Crombouke - No.'s 2 and 3; four in the Rams - No.'s 2, 4, 10 and 12 with three in the Yard - No.'s 3, 4 and 6 as well as a new east development area there. The output per man shift rose steadily during the period from 36.2 cwt. to 44.1 cwt. while the workforce fell from 1575 to 1430 over the same period, the loss mainly being amongst the underground men.

Despite this, the spirit of those at the pit was high. In July 1968, when the majority were on their annual fortnight's holiday, 43 volunteered to return to the pit early in order to keep the East Worsley and West Crombouke districts working. They produced nearly 5000 tons in the process. *Coal News* of September 1968 reported *"Rescue shift win a record 400 more tons a day"*. This referred to the "3 West Crombouke" face which was being worked on a full 24-hour cycle as a result of joint discussions between the men and management over the pit's critical position.

Colliery "target board" at the main entrance to the site.

One of two surviving photographs of the "last shift" taken in April 1970

THE END

However, the writing was on the wall. Astley made headline news in the London Times in April 1969 when the news first surfaced that Astley was threatened with closure. It was described as a "criminal" threat. The proposal went before the Board in June that year, the N.C.B. being "embarrassed" by the rise in productivity at the pit. In the previous year the colliery had actually made a profit.

The pit was reprieved on the 12th. June 1969, but on conditions and the men went in during their July holiday to increase the output. The condition was that before the end of the year the pit had to show an output per man shift of no less than 50 cwt.! To this end the Manager called a number of "Face Conferences" starting with the Worsley No.5 East teams at which representatives for the area, the Unions (including Joe Gormley) met so that everyone including the men, could have their say - but it was, in the end, not enough, and the colliery was deemed uneconomic to operate.

Under these circumstances, it is hardly surprising that the Astley men refused to walk out during the unofficial strike of October 1969, after being visited by 20 miners from Yorkshire. A scene to be repeated at Agecroft Colliery in Salford many years later.

The News Chronicle reported the matter of closure in the following manner:

It's backs to the wall as miners fight pit shutdown - Unless there is a final reprieve, the Lancashire Pit they called "The Last Refuge" will soon be a refuge no longer.   Thousands of people's lives will be disrupted. Since 1912 Astley Green has towered solidly beside the East Lancashire Road. In recent years it has offered jobs to redundant miners as its seven sister collieries fell silent, victims of modernisation, and the slumping demand for coal. It reads like a roll call of the colliery fallen. .. Bedford, Chanters, Cleworth, Gib, Mosley Common, Nook and Sandhole.

Pits which once, with Astley were proudly designated on the May Day banners as "The Tyldesley NUM Branch." After a loss of £600,000 last year, the NCB planned to close Astley Green on June

27th. The date was temporarily deferred after appeals from the National Union of Mineworkers whose delegates will today meet Coal Board officials in Walkden.

There are 17 pits left in the North West compared with 80 just after the war. Since 1959, 345,000 men have left the mining industry. It has been an operation handled with little serious friction so that the death of yet another colliery makes small impact on ordinary folk whose central heating helped condemn it. But the impact in the terraced homes of miners when a colliery stops winding cannot be measured in cold statistics.

The men of Astley Green talked of their future if the Coal Board turns down their plea to give the pit until March to prove itself. Said Les Roberts, 49-year old father of seven, who moved there after 30 years at Mosley Common: "Our backs are to the wall. What the hell are we to do now?" He has been a miner since he was 14 and knows no other job "A future in the coal industry? Say that to a Lancashire man and he'll laugh in your face." Jim Mullin, 34, who lives nearby in Crawford Avenue, complained over the uncertainty, which affects himself and the future of his wife and two sons.

"Even the union officials don't know what's happening. We're beginning to wonder if the Coal Board do. If they are going to close it, let them close it, and we can set about re-forming our lives. My wife Dorothy wants me out of this lot and I can't say I blame her. I'm young enough to train for something else, but there are plenty of over-50's at the pit."

One of them is 58-year-old John Seddon who has worked for more than 40 years in collieries. After a lifetime he faces the prospect of becoming a scrap-heap miner. He said: "Thank God I have no children. For the young it must be very difficult not knowing what is going to happen; where you are going. No-one wants to be on the dole in a land of plenty. But at my age..." If the pit closes, redundancy pay and the search for new jobs will mean a tightening up on family budgets. Underground worker Frank Green, 31, from Wigan, said "A man takes his troubles home, and my wife and I are worried. We will have to give up many of our pleasures, like holidays. There will be fewer nights out, and fewer toys for our three children. My wife may have to go out to work."

Mr Don Sizer, NUM pit secretary, tries to keep up the men's morale. "All we need is 12 months to prove that it is well worth while keeping Astley Green open," he said. "We are trying to encourage the men." Another Union official, 57-year-old Mr John Taylor, area president of the North West Colliery Deputies, insists that the pit is a good one. "To close it would be a tragedy. In rates alone that would cost Tyldesley council £20,000. The men are frustrated because they are being dangled by the NCB."

It was too late. British Rail, one of the largest customers for coal had ceased using coal with the withdrawal of its last steam locomotives in 1968 and so the wet, gassy pits of Lancashire all came under scrutiny, being compared unfavourably in cost terms with the pits in Yorkshire and elsewhere.

Astley Green colliery officially closed in 1970, the last coal being wound in No.1 pit on the 3rd. April. The coal preparation plant continued in use until October, treating coal from other pits on the railway network and for treating coal which had been in stock.

For weeks afterward, however, the winding engines were still at work on site, lifting equipment and winding dirt for backfilling. After the final demolition, only the No.1 shaft headgear and its engine house were left along with the general office and the garage. However, evident for miles were the effects of the colliery's existence; the Bridgewater canal still at its old level, but now surrounded by high banks to support it across the sunken landscape, a mute testimony to the tons of rock removed by Astley's tubs and mine cars.

The shafts were capped and chutes let in to their sides so that slurry from other collieries in the district could be tipped down to help fill the deep shafts. This indignity went on for nearly ten years until the site was vested with a voluntary restoration group. In view of the wholesale closures and the traumas surrounding them in the last few years, it is perhaps difficult today to imagine the feelings then. Perhaps the Astley men were lucky to leave at a time when employment was still high, though it is unlikely they would think so at the time.

Another (damaged) photo of "the last shift" at Astley Green. Taken outside the lamp room in 1970

Demolition of No 2 winding engine. 1970

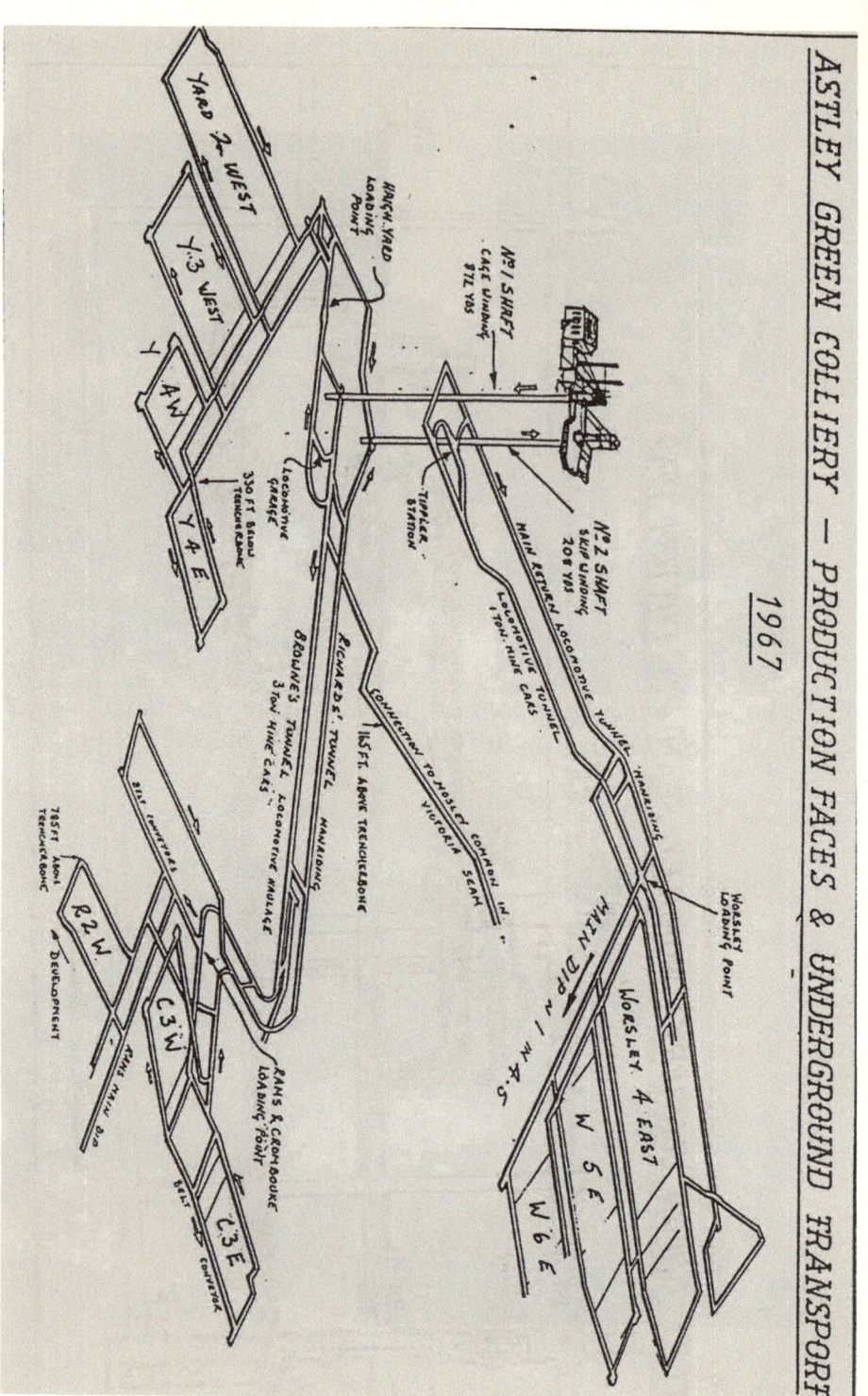

MUSEUM

This could have been the end of Astley Green Colliery, its shafts filled and all traces of the site obliterated to make way for housing or new industry. However, a joint effort by Lancashire County Council, local museum staff, and industrial archaeologists, persuaded the NCB to leave the engine house with its winding engine and headgear for preservation.

During the next ten years the site suffered from neglect and vandalism until in 1980 an agreement was reached between the owners (Greater Manchester Council) and a local group of steam enthusiasts. This gave the Red Rose Steam Society a base to restore equipment they had already collected and also to restore the steam winding engine. The site is now Astley Green Colliery Museum where a collection of mining equipment and examples of steam power are being prepared for display. The engine house and headgear are "Listed Buildings" and will form the focal point of the museum.

Group of Astley Green blacksmiths c1908.

No 2 pulley sheaves ready for raising. 7th May 1916.

No 2 headgear under construction

Ventilation fan being installed.

ASTLEY GREEN COLLIERY NO.1 WINDING ENGINE

INTRODUCTION

The No.1 Winding Engine was the principle winding engine of the colliery. People often comment on seeing it for the first time "why is it so big?" or "how does it work?" The following is a description of both the basic ideas behind the design of winding engines in general, and the Astley Engine in particular. The operations referred to are those which would have been used during the life of Astley Green Colliery.

The purpose of the winding engine was to raise 8 tons of coal every two minutes from the No.1 shaft which was 891 yards deep. The shafts were sunk in 1908 by the Pilkington Coal Company to exploit coal reserves to the south under Astley Moss.

The coal seams dip to the south at about 1 in 5 and outcrop to the north in the Tyldesley area. Coal had been mined there since the 15th century but by the start of the 20th century the only reserves available were deep down to the south. However, such was the demand for coal at this time, that it was considered economic to exploit this coal despite the high cost of shaft sinking and powerful winding engines.

THE ENGINE BUILDERS

The Astley winding engines were designed and built by Yates & Thom Limited of Canal Ironworks, Blackburn. The firm had been established by millwrights William and John Yates in 1826. They built water wheels and a large beam engine and its gearing for the India Mill in Darwen in 1868.

They adopted the Corliss valve in the 1880's and began to use drop valves from around 1900 onward, while they were one of the several manufacturers to adopt the Uniflow engine. They built very large engines for waterworks pumping, for mills, and winding engines for collieries. Most of their records were unfortunately lost in a fire, but it would appear that they had a very great output in the early 1900's, culminating in the construction in the 1911 to 1913 period of the Astley No.1 engine and its near sisters at Askern Colliery, Doncaster. They built their last steam engines in 1938. The Astley Green No.2 winding engine and the boilers were also supplied by Yates & Thom.

The No.1 winding engine cost £9,677

Main bearing casting arriving at Astley Green 1908

INSTALLATION

The engine house was completed by July 1911 and installation of the engine was well advanced by September of that year. In the next image, the group of men are standing in front of the winding drum and to the left and right the main castings are in place.

It is assumed that the 20 ton overhead crane was used for the assembly. Two poor quality photographs exist of the main bearing casting arriving on site. It is understood that it was transported by road, probably using steam traction engines, but unfortunately this cannot be confirmed from the photographs. Transport from Blackburn could have been by road, rail, or canal.

Most parts of the engine are identified by a letter and number stamped into the metal. Even nuts and handrails are marked which suggests that the complete engine was assembled at the manufacturer's works prior to shipping to site.

Group in front of No 1 drum during installation 1908/9

Installation was probably completed in 1912/1913 and it was certainly working by 1915 as can be seen in one of the photographs. Note the pristine condition of the engine and the detailed lining out of the castings.

No 1 engine with engineman at controls 1915

No 1 winding engine in pristine condition in 1915

Overall view of the No 1 Astley Green engine c1954

One side of the Number 1 Winding Engine. The photograph is taken from the top of the winding drum after restoration, and shows Bill Rushbrook busy doing some oiling in 1993!

ASTLEY GREEN COLLIERY No.1 WINDING ENGINE

PLAN VIEW

Not to scale

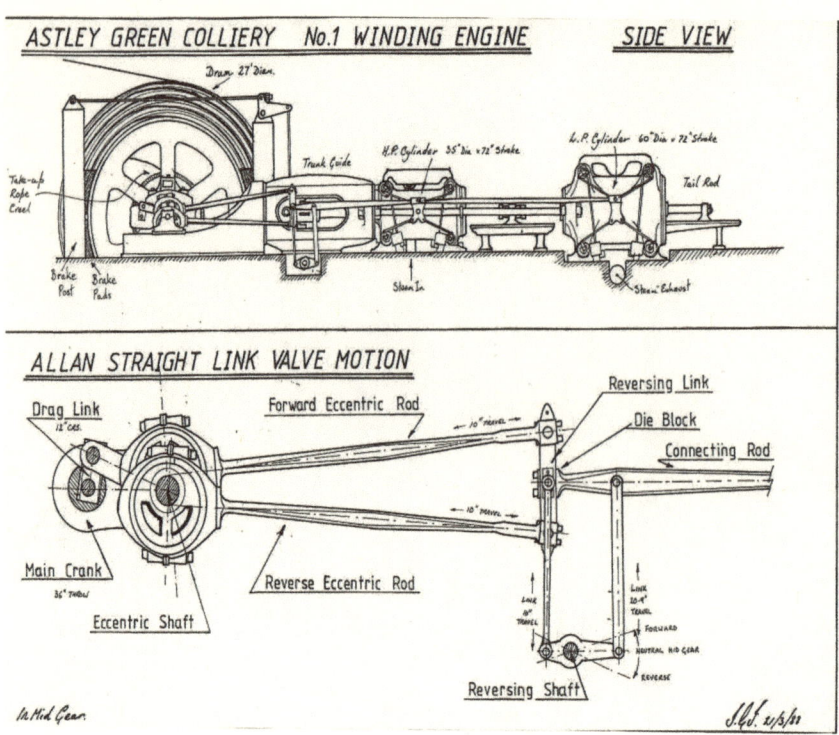

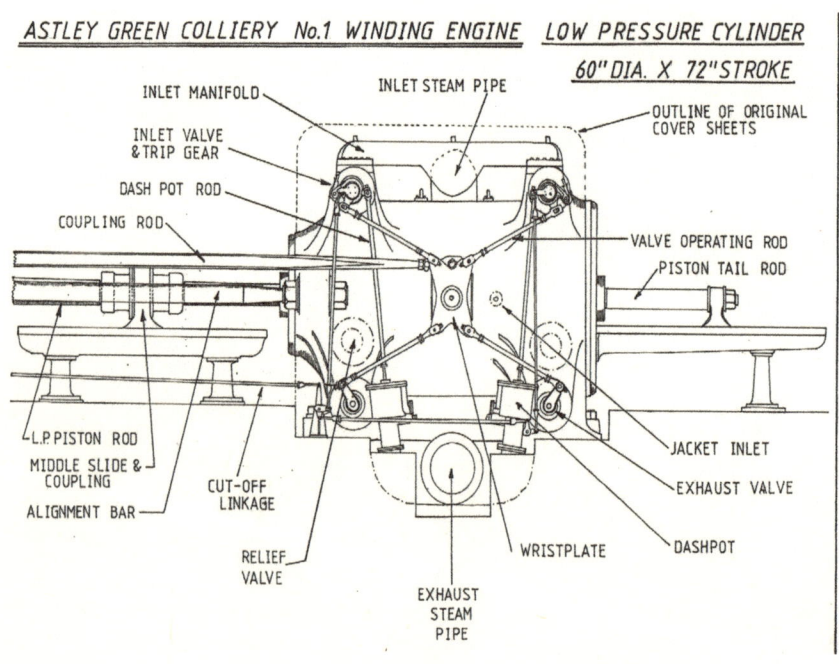

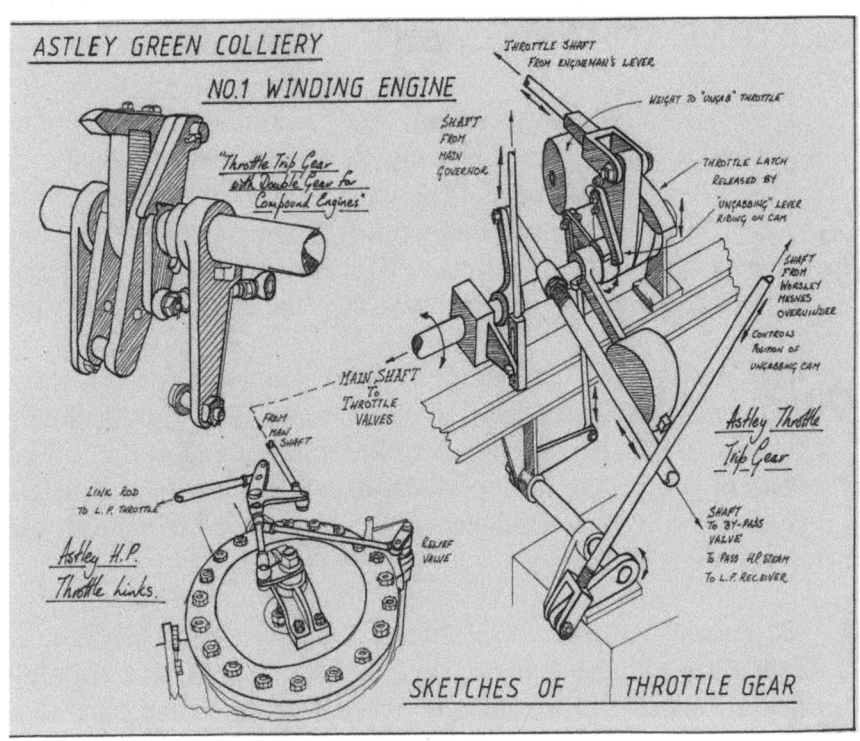

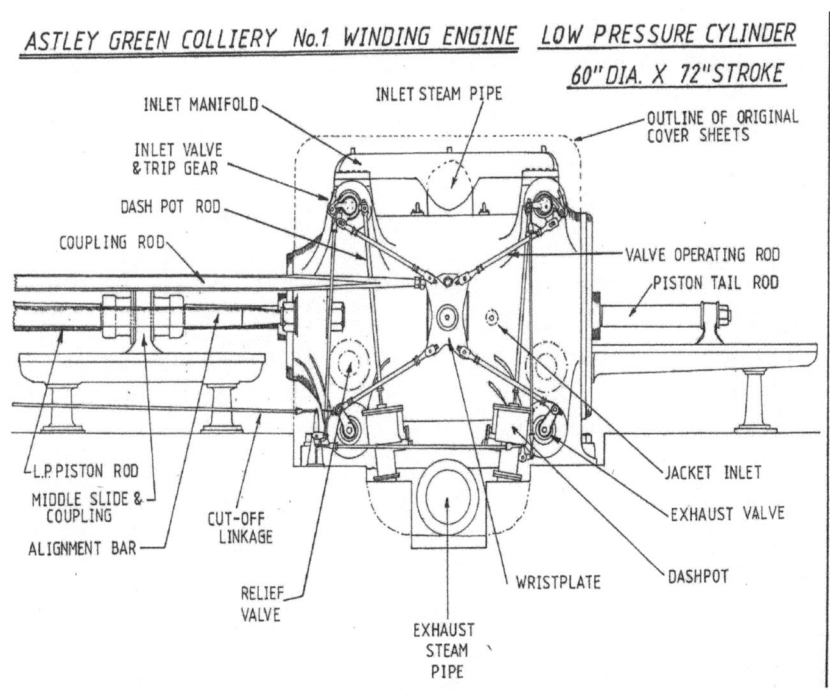

ENGINE ARRANGEMENT

Most steam winding engines had a minimum of two cylinders regardless of their size. This was to ensure that the engine could be started from any position of the cage in the shaft. The piston in each cylinder has a position (dead centre) where no power is transmitted. However by using two cylinders with their cranks set at right angles to each other, one piston could always start the engine from any position.

The Astley No.1 Winding Engine is a twin (or double) tandem compound, that is, the steam was used twice, firstly in the high pressure cylinders, 35 inches in diameter, where it entered at the full boiler pressure of 160 p.s.i. Here it partially expanded, driving the piston in the - cylinder and was then exhausted to a large receiver beneath the engine room floor.

To ensure that there was always a supply of low pressure steam at about 60 p.s.i., the exhaust steam was mixed with a supply of high pressure steam via a reducing valve. This low pressure steam then entered the low pressure cylinders, 60 inches in diameter, where it was again expanded to drive the larger pistons before being exhausted to external accumulators. Thus there are effectively two engines each with their high and low pressure cylinders connected in tandem.

The distance moved by the pistons (the stroke) is 6 ft. The power output of the winder was 3,000 to 3,500 b.h.p., at 57 rpm these being official figures, which were probably exceeded from time to time.

The high pressure cylinders are situated nearest the drum, the low pressure being furthest away. The alignment and security of the cylinders is maintained by stay rods which pass along either side of the cylinders and are clamped to them. The cylinders are all of cast iron construction with cast iron liners.

The pistons are secured by large nuts to the piston rods. The piston rods of both H.P. and L.P. cylinders are connected by middle crossheads which move on and are supported by the middle crosshead slides. This arrangement allows access to both ends of each cylinder, and indeed, allows individual pistons to be withdrawn without requiring the whole engine to be dismantled.

The main crossheads move in massive cylindrical trunk guides which weigh ten tons each. These crossheads transfer the forward and backward movement of the piston rods via the connecting rods to the cranks and thus rotate the drum. A slipper and slide arrangement at the rear of the engine supports the tailrods of the L.P. pistons.

High Pressure Cylinder showing the "wrist plate" and valve assembly.

Each side of the engine is supported by massive brick piers. The castings are secured to the piers by long bolts 2 inches in diameter. At some time several of these bolts were sheared, probably at the same time that the main bearing casting was cracked. Heat loss from the cylinders is minimized by two insulation methods. Firstly a steam jacket is cast into and surrounds the cylinder, and secondly lagging material is placed over this jacket. The cylinders were finished off with planished steel covers which unfortunately rusted away during the period of neglect after closure.

STEAM SUPPLY AND CONTROL

The high pressure superheated steam at 160 p.s.i. required to drive the steam engine was supplied by a bank of 16 Lancashire boilers each 9 ft. in diameter and 30 feet long. These fed the various engines via a 20 inch diameter steam main from which a branch was fed into the No. 1

engine house. A main stop valve provided steam shut off facilities for the main supply when necessary thus isolating the engine from the range.

The piston rods in between the High and Low pressure cylinders.

Water traps were installed at certain vantage points to allow drainage of moisture from the steam lines and to prevent wet steam being carried over into the winding engine throttle valves and cylinders where it could have caused damage. Cylinder lubrication is by mechanical lubricators worked off the high pressure cylinder valve gear.

Speed control of the winder is accomplished by a combination of the movement of the engineman's throttle lever to control the input of steam to the cylinders via the throttle valves and the movement of the brake hand lever and foot pedal controlling the brakes via a steam brake engine. A reversing lever controls the direction of motion of the engine via a steam reversing engine.

The controls are situated on a raised platform along the east side wall of the engine house from which the engineman has a clear view over the whole engine. Access to the platform is now via steps which face towards the low pressure cylinder, although the original arrangement had the steps at the opposite end of the platform.

There are two main throttle valves, one for the low pressure steam control and one for the high pressure steam control. These are situated midway between the respective engine cylinders at just below floor level. The valves are of the Whitmore patent rotary disc type with relief by-pass valves which ensure that they require the minimum effort for manual operation.

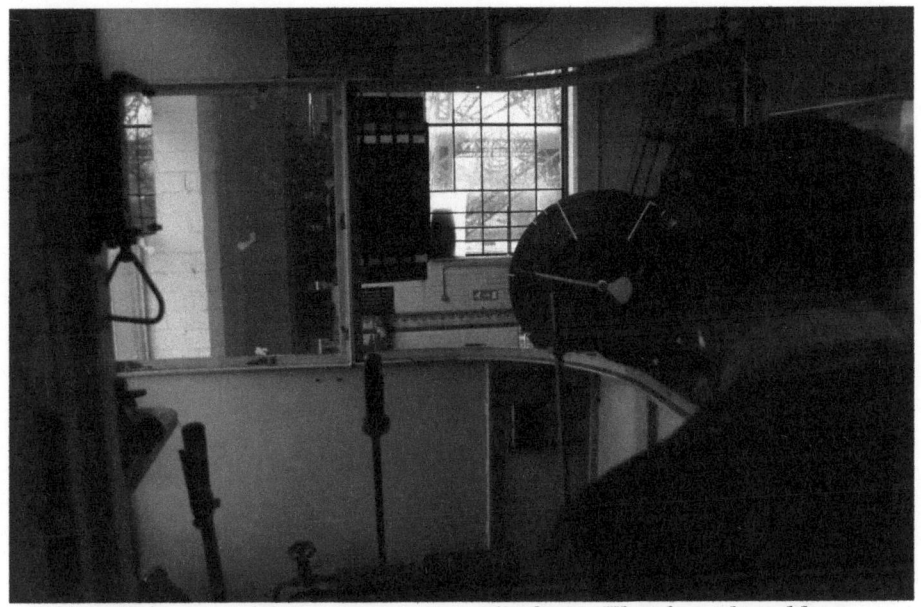

Internal view of the engineman's platform. The three hand levers control the steam pressure, reverse mechanism and brake. There is also a foot brake.

The two throttle valves are linked and are operated by the lever in the control cabin by the winding engineman, the movement being transmitted by a series of linkages to the ungabbing gear. This was also a Whitmore patent, which, in an emergency disengages the throttle lever from the engineman's control and closes the throttle valves automatically by weights. The ungabbing gear is also directly connected to both throttles so that they open and close simultaneously.

WINDING DRUM AND DRIVESHAFT

The simplest and cheapest drum is a plain cylinder with one rope coiling underneath (the underlap or underlay rope) and the other coiling over the top of the drum (the overlap or overlay rope). However, the deeper the shaft the more out of balance the load becomes due to the weight of the rope (each rope for the Astley No. 1 shaft weighs 18 tons).

At some point it becomes cheaper to use other methods than to increase the power of the engine. One method of overcoming this is to attach a balance rope to the bottom of each cage. An alternative method is to use a winding drum which is conical in shape for some or all of its width. At the commencement of the wind from the pit bottom, the rope is arranged to be on the smallest diameter thereby giving greatest lifting force. As the wind progresses the rope moves up the spiral onto larger diameters which provide lower lifting force but greater rope speed. The arrangement of parallel and conical sections on the drum depend on the duty required and a number of types have been produced.

The main winding drum (notice the conical portion at either side). The four upright objects in front of the drum are auxiliary engines, the two outer ones being for the brakes, the left centre one for reversing and the right centre one is the overwinder.

The most common type of conical drum is the bi-cylindro-conical as used on the Astley Green engines. This has a parallel small diameter on which the rope of the ascending cage remains for the initial acceleration of the engine. The rope then starts on the conical section which is arranged to accelerate the cage at a uniform rate to top speed when the rope reaches the large parallel diameter and continues to the end of the wind. The other half of the drum is a mirror image for the other rope.

A consequence of using a conical drum is that for one revolution of the drum the cages will move different distances in the shaft since the ropes are on different diameters. This creates extra complication when loading or unloading cages with more than one deck. One method is to arrange for simultaneous loading of all decks. Astley Green had another arrangement which comprised a hydraulic table at the pit bottom which could be raised and lowered by the Onsetter. Once the cage had landed on the table the engine man and Banksman controlled the position of the cage at the pit bank whist the Onsetter controlled the position of the cage at the pit bottom.

The winding drum is 27 feet in its largest diameter and 17 feet in its smallest diameter, being conical at either end. The drum is of riveted and bolted steel construction, being keyed onto the drumshaft. The drum outer periphery shell plates are lagged with oak blocks on the largest diameter. The cone plates on each side of the drum are fitted with bulb flat sectioned scroll bars riveted onto the cone plate down to the small diameter of the drum. Special lead-in scrolls are provided at the pick up points from the small diameter and also at the lead off points to the large diameter of the drum.

One end of each winding rope is coiled inside the drum onto internal rope reels where the rope end is secured to the inside of the drum structure. This provided spare rope to replace that cut off for the regular test samples. A minimum of three and a half dead laps of the winding ropes were maintained on the small diameter of the drum. There are two winding ropes each weighing 18 tons and 2.365 inches diameter. One was coiled on the left hand side of the drum and passed over the drum and out to the headgear pulley, whilst the right hand rope passed under the drum and out to the other pulley.

The 27" diameter drumshaft is keyed and clamped to the winding drum and supported by pedestal bearings at each side of the drum. These bearings have split-type white metal liners which can be adjusted for wear by a wedge arrangement. The drive is transmitted to the drumshaft via cranks of 3 feet throw, which are a shrink fit on to the drumshaft ends. The cranks are driven via connecting rods from the crossheads on the ends of the piston rods. The drumshaft bearings are lubricated by oil in drip fashion along the whole bearing length from header tanks supported above the pedestals which are replenished by small pumps driven from the eccentric shafts and situated beneath the floor.

The massive casting supporting the bearings are in one piece, each weighing 20 tons 10 cwt. which is 10 cwt. over the capacity of the engine house crane! Clearly they were not intended to be moved very often. The western side casting cracked at some time in the past and was repaired by bolting a steel plate across the fracture which may still be seen today.

VALVE GEAR *(see earlier photo).*
Valve gear is needed to ensure that steam is admitted to and exhausted from the ends of the cylinders in the correct sequence so that the engine operates smoothly and efficiently. The type of valve gear used on this engine is known as Allen's Straight Link Motion. In line with and at each end of the drumshaft are further shafts, known as the eccentric shafts. These shafts are also supported in pedestal type bearings at either end which have adjustable white metal liners.

The twin eccentrics are made of cast iron in two halves and clamped and keyed to the eccentric shafts to ensure the correct steam inlet and exhaust valve opening and closing positions. The drive to the eccentric shafts is by the eccentric shaft crank arm which couples with the main engine crank pins via drag-arm links. This drag-arm maintains a fixed relationship between the drum rotation, piston position and steam inlet and exhaust valve motion. The eccentric straps are also cast iron and are grease lubricated.

The forward-direction eccentric rods are coupled at one end to the eccentric straps and at the other end to the top of the reversing quadrant and the reverse-direction eccentric rods were coupled to the eccentric straps and to the bottom of the reversing quadrant.

A coupling rod from the die block in the reversing quadrant is connected to the wrist plate on the high pressure cylinder and a separate further coupling rod connects the H.P. wristplate with that on the L.P. cylinder to ensure the simultaneous operation of the valves on the two cylinders. The wristplate then operates the inlet and exhaust valves via rods and lever arms.

To change the direction of motion of the engine, the die block is moved from one end of the reversing quadrant to the other, so that the motion of the appropriate eccentric rod is transferred to the coupling rod. The weight of the coupling rods and die blocks is such that power assistance is required to move them in response to the movement of the engineman's reversing lever. This is carried out by a steam operated Reversing Engine mounted in front of the drum. Today we would call this a servo.

INLET AND EXHAUST VALVES

The valves used on the engine are of the "Corliss" semi-rotary type, looking rather like a rolling pin, most of which is cut away - these work in a bored valve cylinder. They have the advantage that they provided a large area of valve which can be opened and closed relatively rapidly only by a slight rotation of the valve itself, the movement being at right angles to the pressure exerted on it by the steam.

On each cylinder the two inlet valves (upper) and the two exhaust valves (lower) are operated by valve rods connected to the wrist plate.

This in turn is coupled to the eccentrics via the reversing link as already described.

When the valve is opened by the valve rod it is latched open by the valve latch. The valve is then retained fully open independently of the continuing movement of the valve rod. Also, opening of the valve lifts the dash pot piston which creates a vacuum beneath it thereby applying a closing force on the valve against the latch. As the valve rod moves towards the exhaust position, at some point the inlet valve latch is tripped by action of the tripping cam operating on the tripping cam rider. Once the latch is tripped the valve closes rapidly under the force of the dashpot.

A low pressure Corliss valve. This particular valve is from Sutton Manor Colliery, St Helens.

The exact point of this cut-off is controlled by the governor which changes the position of the tripping cam independently of the valve rod. The higher the engine speed the earlier the steam is cut off in the stroke. In contrast the exhaust valves are simply opened and closed only by their associated valve rod. They remain open for almost the full length of the stroke to facilitate exhaust steam leaving the cylinder.

THE GOVERNOR

The cut-off is controlled by the speed of the engine. The device used to effect this is the centrifugal governor, situated in front of the drum near the left hand trunk guide, and was originally combined with the overwinder. The governor is coupled directly with the drumshaft by a chain drive which through a worm gear gives rotary motion to the flyweights. As the engine speed increases the flyweights exert more force and move outwards, moving a linkage which passes from the governor along to each engine and then down the outside of the engine to the H.P. & L.P. cylinders and the cut-off tripping mechanisms on the inlet valves. This also helps to limit the maximum speed of the engine.

Control of the cut-off is required to economise on steam. At the start of the wind full steam is required throughout the stoke of the piston to give maximum acceleration to the cage. However once the engine is up to maximum speed the force needed is reduced and this is most efficiently achieved by cutting off the steam part way through the stroke. The steam trapped in the cylinder then expands for the remainder of the stroke.

AUXILIARIES *(see earlier photo of the winding drum)*

On installation, the engine was equipped with a set of auxiliaries by Fraser & Chalmers, of Erith, Kent. These consisted of their own type of steam reversing engine, the steam cylinder being 9" diameter of 18" stroke with a tandem oil cataract cylinder 4.75" diameter of the same stroke, a Whitmore steam brake engine and a Whitmore Patent Overwinder.

The brake engines and the reversing engine are needed since neither motion can be moved by manually. These were mounted in front of the drum, between the crosshead trunk guides. The oil cylinders, in combination with compensating levers ensure that the movement of the brakes and the reversing gear exactly mirror the movement of the engineman's control levers in the driving position.

Brakes

The brakes are of the "post" type, consisting originally of two wooden brake blocks, shaped to match the curvature of a steel brake path, mounted on steel posts. The brake path, some 16" wide and 17 feet in diameter, consists of separate plates mounted clear of the main drum end castings, thus allowing air to circulate around them for cooling purposes.

The posts are mounted on massive pivots at the bottom and linked by steel rods through bell cranks at the top, so that the movement of the bell crank forces the posts towards one another, and pressed the brake blocks against the brake path. Wear of the brake blocks is automatically taken up by a ratchet mechanism which is coupled to the brake operating shaft, thus as the brakes wear, the ratchet is able to advance and rotate a nut on the tie rods, closing up the extra gap between the posts.

In 1954 the original Whitmore brake engine was replaced by a Worsley Mesnes type brake engine in the same location. In 1956-8 a much greater re-arrangement took place when the whole braking and overwinding system was altered. This was occasioned by the changes in the regulations when the Mines Acts were replaced by the single Mines and Quarries Act.

The original Act of 1911 had only required the brakes to be of sufficient power to hold the loaded cage. However, the 1954 Act required the brakes to be capable of holding the cage against the power of the engine - a different thing altogether. The original brake shaft was replaced with two stub shafts at the foot of each brake post. The brake posts were each connected to separate Worsley Mesnes Brake engines positioned in front of them, while below the operating floor, in the basement, two additional engines but without oil cataract cylinders, were connected by levers and cranks to the same brake posts. These replaced the original weights and spring nests with longer springs, the weights now hanging on the new lower engine levers.

The whole system was now arranged to fail to safety in the event of a loss of steam pressure, this being the task of the lower engines whose sole purpose was to keep the weights lifted. Failure of the steam pressure causes the weights to fall, automatically applying the brakes. At around the same time, the wooden brake blocks were replaced by shaped iron castings to which pads of Ferrobestos were bolted on. This allowed an increase of braking force from the 30-35 p.s.i. of the wooden blocks to around 50 p.s.i.

This also much simplified the operation of changing the brakes. With the wooden brake blocks, the replacement of the worn brake blocks had occupied two whole shifts, one for each side of the engine. With a suitable team assembled, and a maintenance shift available - usually Saturday afternoon, or on Sunday, the engineman would balance the empty cages in mid-shaft. Then specially prepared timber props, their ends reinforced with iron would be placed into cut-outs in the masonry engine beds on either side of the drum, and wedged into position so that the drum was firmly supported independently of the brakes. This allowed the engineman to lock the brakes off and relax. Some poor soul then had to shin up to the top of the designated brake post with a large spanner and proceed to unwind the ratchet nut which had been used to take up the wear on the brake blocks.

As the nut unwound, it also wound the brake posts apart, eventually providing enough clearance for the brake blocks to be unbolted and removed and a new set fitted, with the help of the crane. Once the new blocks were in place, the slack on the nut was then taken up by hand, the engineman took up the reins again, the wedges were knocked out and the timbers removed until the next shift, when the other side could be treated similarly. It did not take long after the installation of the Ferrobestos pads for the engineers to realise that it was a waste of time to remove the whole support block to change the pads, as the brakes only needed to be slackened off sufficiently for the old pads to be slipped out sideways and new ones put in. This could be achieved by force of the brake engines alone, and the post shinning exercise was done away with.

Overwinder
The failure of a winding engine to stop (due to either mechanical fault or human error) when the cage arrives at the pit bank has resulted in many accidents particularly in the time before safety equipment. The Overwinder is an independent mechanism which senses that the winding engine is out of control and applies the brakes. The Overwinders have been continually updated as improvements have been devised and they have saved many lives.

The original Overwinder on the No. 1 engine was in front of the left hand brake post, with the reversing engine to its right and the brake engine to the right of that, roughly opposite the centre of the drum. The

Overwinder also acted as governor and controlled the cut-off settings of the inlet valves.

The installation met the requirements of the 1911 Committee on Overwinding prevention, but with later tightening up of mining legislation, the basic form of the Overwinder did not provide complete protection over the whole working range of winding speeds, especially at banking. Thus at some time in the later 1930's, the winder was fitted with an additional Walker-Black type Profile Overwinder, driven from the east side eccentric shaft. This was mounted in an extremely cramped location between the engineman's platform, toilet, engine house wall and the crank ! The Whitmore overwinder was not removed and appears to have supplemented the Walker-Black Device.

In 1956-58 overwind prevention was taken over by a Worsley Mesnes Pneumatic Controller which was located in the old Brake engine position in front of the drum. The Whitmore Overwinder was partially dismantled and reduced to functioning purely as a governor controlling cut-off of the inlet valve. At the same time it was re-located further away from the brake drum, level with the high pressure cylinders.

A small steam driven Westinghouse Air Compressor was also installed in the basement on the engine house wall to provide it with compressed air, presumably to safeguard against a failure of the main colliery air supply. While all this was going on, the entry to the engineman's platform was reversed and the Walker-Black overwinder disconnected.

At closure the inventory recorded the following: In situ; Two Worsley Mesnes Brake Engines 10" x 18"   Worsley Mesnes Pneumatic Controller No. 13225A In store; Worsley Mesnes Brake Engine 10" x 18" No.17339   Walker-Black Overwind Preventer. Which showed that nothing was ever thrown away! Unfortunately, the controllers were removed immediately afterwards, and a complete replacement has taken a long time to find. That now in position was kindly donated by British Coal from Donisthorpe Colliery, in Leicestershire.

The No. 2 Engine had a similar arrangement and went through similar modifications, although not to the same extent as No.1. It was only ever fitted with a single brake engine. At closure, the Brake Engine was a Worsley Mesnes 9" x 14" type, No. 15630, while two reversing engines of the same type Nos. 14305 and 16895 are mentioned - obviously only one was fitted! Again the final overwinder was a Worsley Mesnes Pneumatic type, No. 14401, which had replaced a Walker-Black which was in store.

Winding Ropes

Many types of rope were developed over the years, beginning with hemp, and chains, through flat ropes made from steel wires to a variety of circular steel wire ropes of different constructions. Locked coil ropes were used at Astley - these were made by spinning concentric layers of single wires about a core and finishing with one or more surrounding layers of shaped wires which were inter-locked to restrain the centre layers and to make a smooth cover.

The "locked-coil non-rotating" steel winding cable. The hand belongs to John Lyon!

Depending on the design, one or more of the inner layers were made up of alternate round and shaped or "half-lock" wires, which were designed to lie closely together, thus presenting a smooth surface to the wires in adjacent layers. The outer layers, of fully interlocked wires, were laid on in the opposite direction to the inner layers, with the result that the rope was almost non-spinning. Locked coil ropes were widely employed for winding, especially during sinking pits where their non-spinning character was a great advantage.

The construction was compact and combined flexibility with resistance to losing their shape under load when wound over the head sheaves or on and off the winding drum. Cross-cutting of the internal wires was reduced to a minimum by the arrangement of the concentric layers. The close fitting outer cover of shaped wires had two advantages in that the smooth outer surface reduced abrasive wear, and, in conjunction with a suitable internal lubricant and galvanised wire, the cover helped to prevent internal corrosion of the rope. In addition, broken outer wires were held in position by adjacent wires and might be satisfactorily repaired by running in a short length of new wire and brazing the joints at the ends. When you consider that the winding rope was fully exposed to the elements when it left the engine house to pass up to the pit headgear, then was exposed to more contaminated liquors as it travelled up and down the shaft, it had to be strong, flexible and corrosion resistant!

Every winding rope had to be re-capped at intervals of not more than 6 months at which time 6 feet had to be cut off the length for examination and testing. The cap or capel is a casting which ends in a loop and connects the winding rope to the chains which support the cage or skip. To join the capel to the rope, the various wires which make up the rope are spread out and fused into the structure of the capel by filling it with white metal.

Between the capel and the chains was the detaching hook, which was designed to prevent the cage being wound into the headgear at the top of the shaft by an overwind. In this event, the detaching hook released the winding rope, and special links locked the cage into the headgear until it could be lowered safely. Unfortunately, no-one ever managed to produce a single device which could prevent the cage at the bottom of the shaft plunging into the sump in a similar manner.

WORKING THE WINDER

Let us imagine the situation in the cab, the engineman's position in the winding house, for just one wind. In front of the engine man are two large levers: the steam throttle to the left and the reverser to the right. On his left hand side is the hand lever and latch for the brake. Immediately in front of his seat is the foot pedal for the brake. From the cab the view is dominated by the large shaft signalling board, swung out away from the wall, with to its right the circular face and polished brass pointer of the depth gauge.

Behind the depth gauge is the end of the engine bed and the winding drum itself. The engine has just finished the last of the decking manoeuvres and so the signalling board is dark, apart from the "keps under" light. The depth gauge pointer is close to one end of its travel, opposite the "TB" marker, showing that one cage is at the Trencherbone seam inset - the Pit Bottom.

A pointer close by the drum rim indicates that the bottom most deck of the three deck cage is level with the pit bank. The engine house is almost silent, apart from a background sizzling sound which seems to come from everywhere. The air is hot and humid. The engineman stretches himself his eyes roving constantly over the signalling board as he waits for the off. Suddenly a bell above his head rings one, and on the signaling board the onsetter and raise indicators come on. There is a moments pause and a horn sounds twice, on the board the banksman and lower comes on.

The engineman checks the signals agree, glances at the "MEN/COAL" lamps, of which the "COAL" legend is lit, checks the steam pressure gauge - a good 160 p.s.i. at the throttle valve and then pulls the reversing lever right over to the "REVERSE" position, to lower the cage at bank.

With a hiss and a loud clank, the steam reversing engine in front of the drum operates, moving the massive reversing shaft and the valve gear to their correct positions. He releases the brake pedal and with a smooth motion draws the throttle lever towards him.

Outside the cab the engine begins to move, gradually at first and then with ever increasing speed, hisses and rumbles, the clack of the inlet valves being released, the "swish" of the cranks, all merge into an almost continuous roar. The engineman's attention is on the depth gauge and the pointer which indicates the progress of the wind, with one ear cocked for any out of place sound from the engine in his charge and ready to respond to any signals from the various levels in the shaft. In this case all is well and as the pointer reaches about the half-way point in its travel, he releases the throttle gradually and allows the engine to coast. The engine note changes, as without the sound of the rushing steam, the clack of valves predominates, together with a loud rattle as the valves, no longer held against their seats by steam pressure rise and fall slightly in time with the reciprocating pistons.

Only a quarter of the way to go now, the foot brake is applied, gradually at first and then with more determination as the pointer on the depth gauge approaches the "TB" mark at the opposite end of the gauge. The great drum slows down and the engine man transfers his attention to the marks on the drum rim and their illuminated pointer.

With consummate skill born of long practice and experience, he gently lowers the descending cage on to the hydraulic balance platform at the pit bottom. Meanwhile the top of the ascending cage is level with the pit bank, the engineman now has to use his throttle to bring the cage up to deck level. As each deck is loaded the banksman signals one to the winder to raise the cage to the next deck till all three decks are loaded. The onsetter has complete control of the cage at the pit bottom.

We are now in the situation in which this description began, although the cages have exchanged their locations. From start to finish this winding cycle has taken barely two minutes, 8 tons of coal and about 50 tons of rope, cages and tubs have all moved through half a mile of shaft, accelerated to nearly 60 miles per hour in about 40 seconds and as rapidly decelerated again - to be repeated over and over again, 30 times an hour, 240 times a shift... every day.

This was the work of the winding engine and its engineman. It is a tribute to the winding enginemen of this country, to the engine makers and engineers, to the fitters and the many other skilled trades involved that accidents in shafts have always been headline news, not because they happened very often, but precisely the reverse.

THE OLD DAYS

Visitors are always welcome at Astley, and it is all the more rewarding when they have something to tell us about "the old days" when Astley was a working pit. Unfortunately, with the passing of time memories get hazier, and they need to be put down before they fade altogether. We have been very grateful, therefore, to some of our visitors who have taken the time to chat and allow some of their memories to be written down for posterity. Given time, always at a premium, we hope to be able to do more of this work, as important, in its own way, as the restoration of the No.1 Engine itself.

Overwinds and Output

JIMMY JONES was for many years the surface foreman at the colliery. He recalls two occasions on which the No.1 cages were overwound. Once was at full speed with a full load of coal, the second to test the Overwinder gear. In both occasions the Ormerod Safety Hook operated perfectly. He also recalls an unusual incident when the engine man set off from the surface with the safety keps used for man-riding in position, and several revolutions of the drum were made before it could be stopped. "Imagine the chaos in the engine house ! Being a large rope, it took a full day to sort it out."

Jimmy has also got this to say about the official figures of 30 winds per hour: "Being a banksman at both No.1 and No.2 shafts, I would state that given a steam pressure of 120 psi and a compressed air pressure of 75 psi., the complete cycle of coal winds at No.1 shaft could be 30 to the hour. But everything had to be spot on. Good going considering the depth of shaft, weight of rope, cage, shackles, mine cars and mineral lifted. No.2 was a different kettle of fish as they say, the introduction of skip winding allowing instant loading and discharging at the same time. With less weight and the original deep shaft winder working over a much shorter distance, 60 winds per hour were possible."

A Troublesome Engine

J.W.SAYLES one time District Engineer for the area of the N.C.B. including Astley remembers distinctly two occasions when the No.1 Winding Engine overwound, both times when he was present. On one occasion, as a newcomer to the district and the pit, he had been down to the shaft bottom to inspect the hydraulic table there. He remembers that there was but a single large ram, supporting the table, and working within a cylinder surrounded by water. The weight of the cage and the tubs of coal forcing the ram down and the water up a rising main to a header tank in the Worsley seam (this seems unlikely, he probably meant the next inset above).

Movement of the ram was controlled by a valve in the main under the control of the onsetter. When the cage was raised, the pressure of water was sufficient to return the platform to the level of the pit bottom landing. Having visited this wonder he had returned to the surface and gone across to the Engineers Office to have a bath when the No.1 Engine overwound so violently that the sound was audible all over the pit. So fierce was the impact that the cast iron bell which was intended to catch the detaching hook and retain it in the headgear had smashed and the cage with its full 9 ton load of coal was pulled hard up into the platform of the headgear where it fortunately jammed.

The coal from the 3 mine cars went everywhere and the engineering crew had one hell of a job to release it safely without it joining its partner in the shaft. When it was finally released, it was found that the chain links connecting the detaching hook to the cage proper had all been stretched!

At the foot of the shaft, the impact of the descending cage had been so great that the hydraulic table had been cracked across for some 16 feet. The table was eventually taken out to Walkden Yard where the Metalok company came and metal stitched it. The deck was so long that it could only be stitched a part at a time, the clamps holding it together having to be moved up each time. While the table was being repaired the shaft was worked single sided, the other side cage containing empty cars to help balance the load.

On the second occasion, the engineman was conducting a statutory test of his safety gear, with the Colliery Engineer and District Engineer in the cab with him. Unfortunately, although he was, in Sayles' opinion, one of the most senior of the winding enginemen, he was trying too hard to hear what the two engineers were saying and not concentrating on what he was doing. Thus when he overwound, causing the Walker Black overwinder to trip out he re-set it and without thinking, set off in the same direction again, with predictable consequences! One cage was latched up into the headgear, the cable coming in-house with some violence.

It was these accidents, the latest of many, which were instrumental in getting the powers that be moving to have the Walker Black replaced with a more effective device.

Mr. Sayles was of opinion that the No.1 Engine gave the engineers more headaches than all the others in the District put together. One problem was the brakes, especially after the new installation of 1955-6. A "normal" load on the brake path was thought to be 40 p.s.i. but that at Astley was no less than 80 p.s.i. and when working a maximum unbalanced load at start and end of shift the brake paths became considerably overheated and when they shrank, they set. This led to too-frequent breaking of the bolts which held the brake path onto the main castings. This trouble was never cured despite the attentions of the best that the N.C.B. could provide.

Mr Sayles also believes that, following the conversion to hauling mine cars, the engine was overloaded for when it started it wound well up the first part of the scroll until the governor cut in and lengthened the cut off. The engine immediately slowed down and began to labour, the governor cut out again, restoring full steam, until the cable reached the main part of the drum and the cages had passed one another then it cut in again normally. (It may be significant that in later years the engine appears to have worked with live steam for most of the stroke and the governor did little.).

He recalled that the substantial cost of the Methane drainage scheme to remove the gas from the workings was saved in fuel bills in only 12 months. The range supplied some 2,800 cfm. to the boilers at a suction pressure of some 13 inches of Mercury. This itself caused some little difficulty as the flame safety device which was designed to detect an explosive mixture in the range and vent it off kept tripping. Only after extensive testing was it discovered that it was designed to work on a maximum suction pressure or 8 inches, not 13!

He also remembers an occasion when the brake rod(s) on the east side of No.1 Engine broke when man carrying with 120 men in the cages. The engineman, with great presence of mind, put the engine into reverse and balanced the cages before bringing it up gradually to bank.

PRESERVATION

When the colliery closed in 1970 No.1 winding engine could have followed the same fate as many others and have been cut up for scrap. However the historical importance of the engine was known to local museum staff and to officers in Lancashire County Council. Fortunately they pursuaded the NCB to leave the engine and its associated headgear intact for preservation. However it was not until some ten years later when a group of volunteers (now the Red Rose Steam Society) joined forces with Greater Manchester Council to restore the engine. By that time both the engine and the engine house had suffered the combined ravages of weather and vandals. GMC obtained grants from the EEC and restored the fabric of the engine house, painted the headgear, and secured the site.

Red Rose were able to obtain some replacement parts for the engine from a sister engine at Askern Colliery (now demolished) near Doncaster courtesy of the NCB. However it was not until the mid 1980s that restoration began in earnest on the engine. The aim of the restoration is to return the engine to steam again so that it can be best appreciated by future generations.

View over the Astley Green Stockyard in 1960's

Transport at Astley Green Colliery.

When Astley Green Colliery first opened, there were few transport links to the pit except for the canal and rather poor roads. The canal loading basin used earlier by the Tyldesley Coal Company at Astley Green was purchased for £600 in October 1913. This was located at the south-eastern end of the Astley Green site.

Coal was carried on the canal in box boats. These were horse drawn boats containing 20 tons of coal in 10 wooden boxes. The boxes were filled at the colliery and taken to the canal wharf by flat rail wagons. Here they were lifted into the boats by steam crane. Most of the coal was sold to power stations such as Trafford Park and Stretford. The boxes would be lifted out and the coal discharged from hinged doors at the base of the box.

One horse would haul two boats. The captain would steer one and two lads took turns leading the horse or steering the other boat. The box boat traffic ceased in 1952 after a 200 year history. However, one box boat named "Fred" was fitted with a 2L2 Gardner engine in 1942 and this boat survived and was on display at Astley Green museum until vandals destroyed it.

A steam crane loading a box of coal onto a barge at Astley.

To facilitate the transport of coal, a private railway line was constructed from the colliery, passing across the canal and part of Astley Moss to join the LNWR railway near to Astley Station. The line was 1.5 miles in length and due to the nature of the land, the line was constructed on a base of tree trunks, brushwood to provide a "floating foundation" on top of the boggy land and with a topping of mining spoil. The line was fairly flat apart from the steep climbs up to the canal bridge which made locomotives work hard with their loads of coal, or slurry for the tip.

The locomotive ASTLEY was purchased by Pilkington Collieries Ltd in 1908 from Peckett & Sons of Bristol and was used not only at the colliery itself but also in the construction of the line across the Moss. This loco was a four coupled saddle tank, class M5 and remained at Astley Green until being sold to Craven Brothers of Reddish around 1936.

Steam cranes on the wharf

Strengthening the Whitehead Hall road bridge c 1908

The loco ASTLEY bring used in the construction of the private line connecting the colliery with the LNWR line south of the canal. The rail foundations can clearly be seen.

ASTLEY in August 1908 with the Lancashire boilers in the background and the temporary headgear.

In the early days, local coal deliveries were initially by horse and cart. The cart carries the "Pilkington Colliery Company" name which was set up by the Clifton & Kersley Coal Company.

Over the years, a variety of different locomotives were used at Astley Green, some being based permanently there but others were used on the wider network of colliery lines in the area. Some of those known to have operated at Astley Green are listed below:

ASTLEY   Purchased as new in 1908

WINNIE   Bought in 1911 from Thomas Mitchell of Bolton

The loco WINNIE with the temporary engine shed to the rear.

OUTWOOD   Transferred from Outwood Collieries Ltd in 1912

ASTLEY GREEN   Purchased from J F wake, Darlington in 1914

EDWARD   Purchased as new, date unknown

BLACK DIAMOND   Transferred from Clifton & Kersley Coal Company in 1922

NEWTOWN   Transferred from Clifton & Kersley in 1928

CERBERUS   Transferred from Central Railways system prior to 1936

The loco ASTLEY GREEN

The loco's BLACK DIAMOND (front) & STANLEY (rear) in front of the locomotive shed at Astley Green in 1922.

STANLEY	Transferred from Central Railway system c 1933
BEDFORD	Transferred from Bedford Colliery c 1933
CARBON	Transferred from Atherton Collieries in 1938
FRANCIS	Transferred from Central Railways system c 1945
HUMPHREY	Purchased by Manchester Collieries in 1946

This volume is really concerned with the colliery itself, but for anyone interested in the railways and trains of this area, you should try to get hold of a copy of "The Industrial Railways of Bolton, Bury and the Manchester Coalfields" Part 2 by Townley, Appleton, Smith & Peden, an absolutely stunning volume without which I couldn't even begin to write about the rail transport of Astley Green. Thanks 'fellas!

Over the years the rail sidings developed at Astley Green and in 1932 a new private line opened between the colliery and the Boothsbank loading basin at Boothstown *(illustrated below)*. This new line now linked Astley Green to a reversal point and extensive sidings at Ashtons Field Colliery near Little Hulton – and from there reversal took one to Linnyshaw Moss Sidings about a mile away.

In the March 2003 issue of the "Industrial Railway Record" (the bulletin of the Industrial Railway Society -http://www.irsociety.co.uk/), Steve Leyland reveals some interesting facts about one of the local rail links which existed in the late 1960's when he was lucky enough to be allowed on the locomotive footplates. His comments are reproduced below:

"Power station coal was the staple commodity of Astley Green at this time and that bound for Kearsley made the longest trip to British Rail via Ashtons Field.

The first 1.1 miles from the pit, straight and virtually level, mostly ran parallel with the Bridgewater Canal. At the taxing left hand curve at Booths Bank, the railway crossed the 100 foot contour and trailed into the original line, which went straight down to Boothstown (or Booths Bank) canal basin.

Facing more or less north for the next 2.8 miles, the adverse gradient averaged 1 in 54 until the 300 foot contour was reached near the top of Walkden Bank. As with many NCB lines, the severity varied greatly within that distance, but quite a lot was at about 1 in 30.

The route through Boothstown, under the East Lancs Road, by the closed Mosley Common Colliery, and under the former LNWR Leigh loop line (still open until May 1969) to north of Ellenbrook demanded less arduous work from the locomotives.

The ex Lancashire and Yorkshire High Level line loomed ahead on its embankment and bridges. It was now tough going as far as the Walkden Workshops, before a brief respite preceded the formidable Walkden Bank itself, 0.7 of a mile from the town centre.

A kink to the right, one third of the way up, marked the start of the marginally steepest pitch of 1 in 18 according to my estimate (officially 1 in 24).

Via Ashtons Field, the distance from Astley Green Colliery was 3.9 miles, and the journey took 22 to 25 minutes, depending on circumstances"

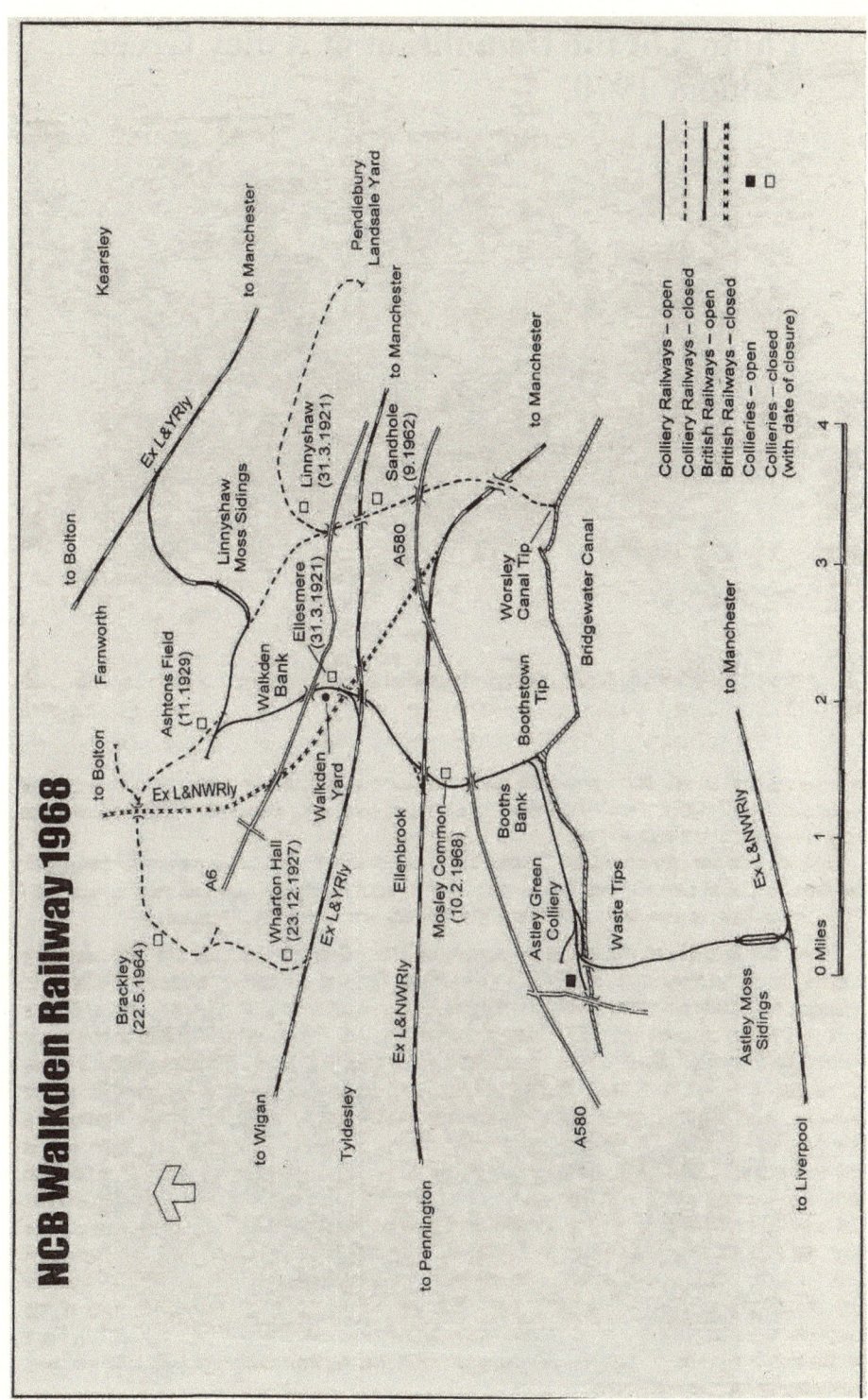

Photo's of the Demolition of Astley Green Colliery 1970.

Demolition of No 2 with No 1 headgear still visible at the left

No 2 during demolition.

The garage during the demolition.

Fan evacees during demolition

No 1 pit bank at the time of demolition.

Number 1 – looking from No 2 – during demolition.

No 1 Capstan House being demolished with the "saved" Engine House on the left.

The end of the working colliery!

Colliery Facts in 1967

Area of colliery surface.   42 acres
Workable Reserves.   65,250,000 tons
Planned saleable output.   3,000 tons per day
                             Or 732,000 tons per year
Dip in seams   1 in 5

The two shafts are No 1 (Downcast) and No 2 (Upcast) with a connection in the Victoria seam to Mosely Common Colliery.

No 1 shaft.
The shaft is 21 feet in diameter and is 890 yards deep. The upper portion is lined with tubbing where it passes through water bearing strata, otherwise the shaft is bricklined.

The headgear is of steel lattice design and the winding engine is a steam, Twin tandem compound engine built in 1912.

The cages have three decks each to carry one 3 ton capacity car with a capacity of 270 tons per hour. The shaft winds from 872 yards depth and handles coal, men and materials to the Crombouke, Rams and Yard seams.

No 2 shaft.
The shaft is 21 feet in diameter and is 833 yards deep.

The shaft is used for coal winding in the upper 283 yards and the lower section is fitted with an auxiliary winder.

The headgear is of steel lattice design and the winding engine is a steam single cross compound engine built in 1913. The shaft is fitted with two 6 ton skips with a capacity of 300 tons per hour and winds coal from the Worsley seam.

Ventilation.
A new fan was put into commission in June 1965 replacing the earlier modified Walker Macard adjustable pitch axial flow fan. The new fan

is a 177 inch Davidson "Sirocco" single inlet, backward Aerofoil bladed fan driven by a 2,100 HP Synchronous Induction Motor through a gearbox.

Methane Drainage.

The drainage of methane from the strata surrounding the faces is being carried out on a large scale with gas being collected and piped to the surface at the rate of 1,624,000 cu ft per day/pure methane. Surface plant measures and controls the gas before it is passed to the steam raising plant.

At the present time six of the Lancashire boilers, and the water tube boiler are equipped for burning methane and this saves the burning of some 480 tons of coal per week.

Power Plant.

There are 14 Lancashire Boilers in use and of these:
    Two are fitted with Chain Grate Stokers.
    Six are fired with pulverized fuel.
    Six are equipped for burning methane. *(nearest the camera in the photo)*

All boilers steam at 160 lb/sq in and the plant is fitted with two banks of Greens Economisers.

In addition to the above, a Water Tube Boiler fired with a Martin Stoker has been erected :-
1. In order to burn slurry from Astley Green and surrounding collieries.
2. For increased efficiency thus effecting a substantial saving in operating cost.

Coal Preparation Plant.

Comprising - Dense medium plant (using magnetite) treating 8" x 1" and Baum Plant treating 1" x 0

Total rated capacity 300 tons per hour.

The R.O.M. coals from No. 1 shaft (Rams, Crombouke and Yard Seams), and No. 2 Shaft (Worsley Seam only) are conveyed separately to respective primary screens sizing at 8" with the + 8" admixing onto a plate picking belt. Inferior coal is passed to a crusher and joins the No. 1 pit minus 8" and the dirt, is ploughed into wagons.

The respective raw coals 8"- 0" are bunkered separately via twin tripper conveyors (2 bunkers to each quality) with a total capacity of 1,600 tons, and are withdrawn at a controlled rate. Worsley coal is screened at 1" producing Dry Smalls for direct sale, and the 8" x 1" is admixed with the 8"-0" (No. 1 Pit Seams) and fed at 300 T.P.H. to the washery.

Screening is effected at 1" and the 8" x 1" is fed to a pre-wetting screen with final delivery into a Drewboy dense medium primary bath operating at 1.4 Sp.Gr. Cleaned coal is paddled out onto drainage and spray screens and classified at 3" and 1.5". Sinks material is withdrawn ' and passed into a secondary bath operating at 1.7 Sp.Gr. The floats after draining and spraying are crushed and join the No.1 Pit 8"-0" feed to the bunkers.

The final sinks are drained and sprayed and delivered to a dirt conveyor common to both the dense medium and Baum sections.

Dry smalls: 1" x 0" is further screened at 5/8" producing No.1 Pit dry smalls at 5/8"-0 for direct sale, and the 1" x 5/8" delivered to a 100 ton surge bunker feeding the Baum plant. The degree of extraction can be varied to meet varying market demands for dry or washed smalls, and facilities exist to produce a blend of dry/washed smalls.

Cleaned coal from the Baum washbox is laundered to screens sizing at 5/8" and the 1" x 5/8" is admixed with 1.5" x 1" from the dense medium section. Washed coal 5/8"- 0" is laundered over fixed sieves and directed into centrifuges and the centrifuged smalls are conveyed to a 30 ton bunker for outloading.

Water clarification equipment is also incorporated producing an uncleaned filter cake for consumption on the Martin stoker.

The grades produced are all loaded into rail wagons and comprise:

Hand Cleaned Larges	+ 8"
Washed Cobbles	8" x 3"
Washed Trebles	3" x 1.5"
Washed Smalls	5/8" – 0"
No.1 Pit Dry Smalls	5/8" – 0"
Worsley Dry Smalls	1" – 0"
Filter Cake	0.5mm – 0"

Surface Control Room
The control room is adjacent to the lamproom and telephone exchange and contains the Electronic Line Signalling and Indicating Equipment (E.L.S.I.E.).

The display consols show the underground layout and whether the conveyors and power loaders are running or not, and the running times of all these items are continuously recorded. These records being used at the daily production meetings.

The control room is manned by a 'controller' who is in direct telephonic communication with underground and where delays and stoppages occur he is able to contact the appropriate official so that remedial action can be taken. The controller is also able to give the manager a complete report on every district at any given time, or draw his attention to any matter which may require his attention.

Apart from monitoring machinery, E.L.S.I.E has been extended to cover safety aspects, such as volume of airflow in the return airways and smoke detectors and also the remote control and monitoring of the main pumps and lodges underground.

Underground Transport
The main transport system consists of locomotive tunnels 17 feet wide and 13 feet high equipped with double tracks of 60 lb/yard rails at 2 feet gauge.

Locomotives are Diesel 100 H.P. single cab type and the mine cars are of 3 tons capacity with Willison ¾ couplings. Man riding is provided using 50 H.P. Diesel locomotives and Wickham cars each carrying twenty-four men.

The secondary transport system consists of belt conveyors to central loading stations. There is one loading station in No. 2 Pit for loading Worsley coal and two loading stations in No. 1 Pit. One of these is in the Southern Area for loading Crombouke and Rams coals and the other to the North of the shaft for loading Yard seam coal.

Production.
Output is at present being obtained from 4 faces, one is in the Worsley seam and three in the Yard seam, with a standby face in the Crombouke seam and development districts in the Crombouke and Rams seams.

Powered supports are installed on the Worsley 5 East face and the Crombouke 2 South East Standby Face. A further set of powered supports is available for the 3 West Crombouke face when it comes into production.

The colliery is currently producing 2,800 ton of Saleable coal per day at an O.M.S of 40 cwt.

All the above is taken from an NCB Brochure of 16th October 1967

Red Rose Steam Society.

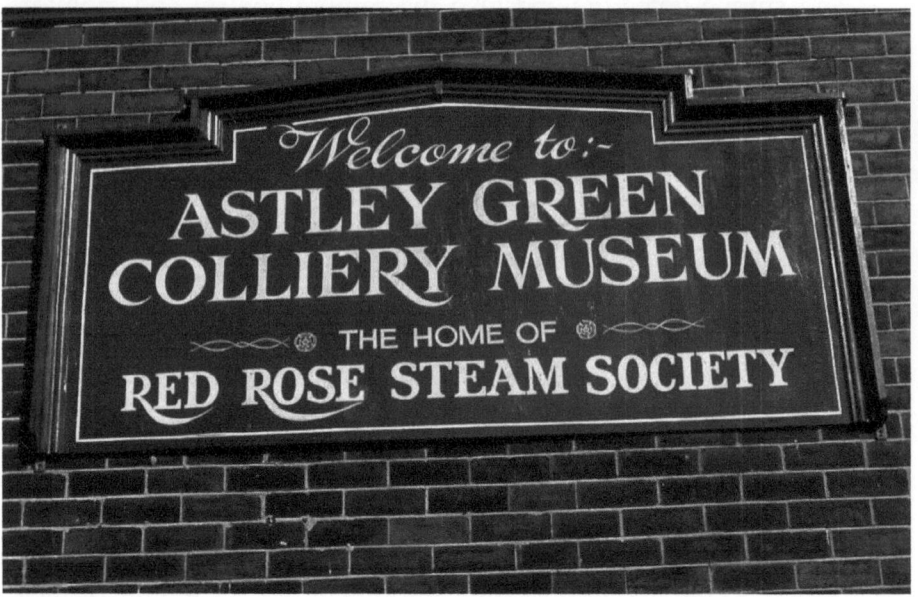

When Astley Green Colliery closed in 1970, the National Coal Board started to demolish the whole site and remove everything that was there - as was the norm with other closed collieries. Luckily, local history museums, industrial archaeologists plus Lancashire County Council managed to persuade the NCB not to destroy the No 1 Winding Engine House with its contents and the headgear.

The site was saved ...... or was it? Unfortunately, just saving a site from destruction doesn't necessarily "save" it and for the next ten years, the remains of the colliery lay derelict and suffered from total neglect and vandalism.

The Red Rose Steam Society was formed in 1972 by a group of steam enthusiasts at Standish, their aim being to save some of the rapidly vanishing examples of steam power in the area. Although the power house and headgear at Astley Green had been saved from demolition, there was no real "custodian" of the site until the late 1970's when the new owners, Greater Manchester Council, signed a lease with the Red Rose Steam Society who then moved on to the site in 1979.

GMC managed to obtain grants for Astley Green Colliery to restore the fabric of the engine, painting of the headgear and landscaping the whole site. Red Rose created a workshop and clubroom in a derelict building which was due for demolition, and began the long slow task of trying to restore the No 1 winding engine.

Following the re-organisation of local government, Wigan Council took over the ownership of the site and they together with Red Rose Steam Society plan to create a museum based around the Winding House and headgear. The aim is to illustrate the history of mining and steam power and to show, using working equipment, the importance that coal and steam power had in the development of British Industry, and the associated engineering excellence which made this possible.

Although the Steam Society has now been at the site for many years, there are decades of work yet to be done. The plans for the future of the colliery are wide and varied but large amounts of money and many man hours of work will be needed to bring them to fruition.

The site of Astley Green Colliery is something worth preserving for future generations. It is part of our history of the North West and graphically illustrates the ingenuity, engineering expertise, bravery and hard work of those entrepreneurs at the start of the 20th century. The remains at Astley Green are a standing monument and reminder of our past, and should be treasured as something precious and worth keeping for future generations. To allow the engine house and headgear to fall into disrepair would be criminal.

To preserve the site will entail careful planning and help by all parties involved, from the local community, Red Rose Steam Society, local authorities, local businesses and those who help dispense public funds for worthwhile projects. Please help to protect OUR heritage and history.

If you are interested in ensuring the future of the Colliery and want to know what YOU can do to help, then please contact the Red Rose Steam Society at Astley Green Colliery Museum, Higher Green Lane, Astley, Manchester M29 7JB.

List of surface workers at Astley Green around April 1970 prior to final closure.

PAY NUMBER	NAME	OCCUPATION	DATE OF BIRTH
3023	H LATHOM	No 1 WINDING ENGINEMAN	14.07.1917
3047	H HILL	No 1 WINDING ENGINEMAN	31.05.1922
3003	H OWEN	No 1 WINDING ENGINEMAN	13.04.1911
3005	R BAILEY	No 2 WINDING ENGINEMAN	27.03.1922
3011	A HILL	No 2 WINDING ENGINEMAN	27.03.1913
3009	C FAIRHURST	No 2 WINDING ENGINEMAN	24.03.1923
3006	T GOULD	FAN ATTENDANT	21.05.1916
3013	A BERRY	FAN ATTENDANT	16.09.1909
3026	R HALL	FAN ATTENDANT	22.03.1911
3034	L PEMBERTON	FAN ATTENDANT	03.03.1908
3017	H FRICKER	No 1 POWERHOUSE ATTENDANT	23.01.1905
3018	W PARKINSON	No 1 POWERHOUSE ATTENDANT	05.10.1910
3041	J WEBLEY	No 1 POWERHOUSE ATTENDANT	12.08.1923
3036	L SPOORMANS	No 2 POWERHOUSE ATTENDANT	30.10.1915
3048	S LEATHERBARROW	No 2 POWERHOUSE ATTENDANT	26.01.1912
3369	W SUTTON	No 2 POWERHOUSE ATTENDANT	15.01.1910
3024	J YATES	No 1 OPERATOR W.T.BOILER	10.11.1919
3030	D NORRIS	No 1 OPERATOR W.T.BOILER	01.07.1916
3043	A GERRARD	No 1 OPERATOR W.T.BOILER	05.04.1905
3051	J CHADWICK	No 2 OPERATOR W.T.BOILER	22.12.1919
3049	J KELLY	No 2 OPERATOR W.T.BOILER	18.15.1925
3273	E DAVIES	No 2 OPERATOR W.T.BOILER	02.08.1937
3025	F WHITTLE	No 3 OPERATOR W.T.BOILER	16.09.1907
3052	L WHITTON	No 3 OPERATOR W.T.BOILER	20.01.1917
3012	W PARRY	No 3 OTERATOR W.T. BOILER	13.10.1923
3031	E DELUCE	TELPHER CRANE DRIVER	29.04.1927
3044	J CASSIDY	TELPHER CRANE DRIVER	21.10.1936
3032	A YATES	WAGON TRIMMER W.T.B.	18.01.1913
3033	T WILLIAMS	WAGON TRIMMER W.T.B.	01.11.1919
3220	A HARRISON	BUNKER GRID W.T.B.	05.11.1919
3075	W CATTERALL	BUNKER GRID W.T.B.	06.05.1915
3085	A WOOD	WATER TREATMENT	04.01.1935
3035	V JORDAN	LANCASHIRE BOILERS	18.08.1916
3235	J MANNING	LANCASHIRE BOILERS	22.10.1924
3008	J CUNLIFFE	LANCASHIRE BOILERS	30.12.1926
3046	P URMSTON	BOILER SCALER	17.06.1910
3038	G CLOUGH	BOILER SCALER	22.10.1908
3363	J NEWTON	SPARE MAN W.T.B.	23.06.1909
3039	J GRUNDY	MARTEN STOKER CLEANER	01.07.1909
3329	J A HOLMES	ENGINEERS CLERK	10.09.1924
3417	R CORRIGAN	CLERK MARTEN STOKER W.T.B.	07.04.1907

PAY NUMBER	NAME	OCCUPATION	DATE OF BIRTH
3019	T RUSSELL	FOREMAN BLACKSMITH	29.10.1922
3097	W BIMPSON	CHARGEMAN BLACKSMITH	10.11.1917
3106	J BELLERBY	BLACKSMITH	08.10.1919
3096	W PENDLEBURY	BLACKSMITH	10.06.1927
3104	J PROUDLOVE	BLACKSMITH	05.03.1947
3056	A BOWDEN	BLACKSMITH	28.08.1919
3101	A CHADWICK	BLACKSMITH	06.05.1912
3111	F TUFFIN	BLACKSMITH	23.10.1923
3102	A SHEPHERD	BLACKSMITH	25.12.1942
3113	A GREGORY	BLACKSMITHS STRIKER	03.01.1923
3110	H BRIDGE	BLACKSMITHS STRIKER	15.03.1928
3014	S HAMER	BLACKSMITHS STRIKER	21.01.1921
3114	J GILL	BLACKSMITHS STRIKER	18.01.1912
3107	H BROWN	BLACKSMITHS STRIKER	03.04.1906
3065	R LITTLER	MECHANIC IN CHARGE	14.06.1916
3089	J WILLIAMS	MECHANIC IN CHARGE	20.08.1926
3103	H TOMLINSON	MECHANIC IN CHARGE	30.01.1911
3079	F GILL	MECHANIC IN CHARGE	31.07.1921
3061	G GREGORY	FOREMAN MECHANIC	29.06.1903
3108	J TURNER	MECHANIC	09.02.1933
3078	R TAYLOR	MECHANIC/TURNER	19.08.1924
3063	H SIMPSON	TURNER	26.10.1909
3084	T RATCLIFFE	MECHANIC	01.06.1912
3081	C GRAHAM	MECHANIC	24.07.1938
3069	N LYTH	MECHANIC	07.01.1931
3082	G PLATT	MECHANIC LANCS BOILERS	31.01.1913
3105	G HUDSON	MECHANIC W.T.B.	06.11.1938
3098	E NEAL	MECHANIC C.P.P.	26.11.1913
3116	F MEREDITH	MECHANIC C.P.P.	29.10.1909
3290	J TURNER	MECHANIC C.P.P.	09.01.1915
3080	F MORT	MECHANIC C.P.P.	13.11.1912
3149	J GREEN	DRILLER	24.10.1926
3058	T DAINTON	BIT GRINDER	29.01.1911
3140	S SPRUCE	WELDER	28.07.1933
3141	W CANNING	WELDER	19.01.1921
3067	W RIGBY	WELDER	09.04.1917
3128	J HOPE	JOINER	01.09.1907
3094	D CLOUGH	JOINER	25.10.1944
3126	T BROWNLOW	PAINTER	23.03.1916
3166	A JONES	PAINTER	08.06.1910
3132	T MERRILL	BRICKSETTER	18.11.1910
3133	J COLLIER	BRICKSETTER	07.05.1922
3134	P MORT	BRICKSETTER	12.06.1916
171	F GREEN	SHAFTMAN	15.11.1924
176	F HARTLEY	SHAFTMAN	05.09.1926
175	J HIGGINS	SHAFTMAN	28.01.1911
177	R RATCLIFFE	SHAFTMAN	10.04.1906
178	A SACKFIELD	SHAFTMAN	27.12.1909
179	J OWENS	SHAFTMAN	01.02.1920

PAY NUMBER	NAME	OCCUPATION	DATE OF BIRTH
3190	J HILL	ASST BANKSMAN	26.07.1919
3192	R MAYOH	BANKSMAN	28.01.1910
3193	E TIMPELLEY	COAL PREP PLANT	07.03.1911
3194	A HOLLAND	BANKSMAN	28.03.1908
3195	W FAIRHURST	ELECTRICIAN NIGHTS	03.03.1946
3196	S CUNLIFFE	C.P.P.	27.06.1909
3197	H CHIVERS	MINE CAR CONTROL No1 PIT BANK	10.10.1914
3199	J ROWSON	FEEDER ATT No1 PIT BANK	16.06.1916
3202	J T MARSH	MESSENGER AND CLEANER	07.07.1930
3203	J WOODS	MINE CAR CONTROL No1 PIT BANK	08.06.1914
3204	E CARDEN	C.P.P.	13.09.1910
3205	J MERCER	GENERAL WORKER NIGHTS	01.08.1916
3206	P BENT	CHARGEHAND POWDER MAGAZINE	11.12.1910
3207	D BOWDEN	FEEDER ATT No2 PIT BANK	23.02.1937
3212	T GOULDEN	GENERAL WORKER NIGHTS	10.07.1909
3214	I LEWTCHENKO	C.P.P.	06.06.1920
3216	J LYON	BANKSMAN	05.03.1907
3218	A HARPER	BANKSMAN	04.10.1930
3219	E WILLIAMS	TELEPHONE OPERATOR	25.02.1908
3222	J GALLAGHER	CHARGEHAND PIT BANKS NIGHTS	26.03.1913
3223	J ELSBY	POWDER MAGAZINE ATTENDANT	03.06.1917
3225	JIMMY L JONES	SURFACE FOREMAN	18.01.1913
3233	J THORPE	C.P.P.	22.10.1015
3234	F STRINGER	C.P.P.	25.12.1931
3236	R JOHNSON	LOCOMOTIVE STOKER	28.05.1909
3237	W MILLARD	GENERAL WORKER	28.11.1915
3238	J TURNER	C.P.P.	13.10.1919
3239	D CONNOR	FEEDER ATT No1 PIT BANK	17.11.1`909
3240	J GARDNER	CHARGEHAND PIT BANKS AFTS	17.04.1910
3241	T WRIGHT	C.P.P.	18.02.1914
3245	A HEYES	DITCHING	01.06.1908
3249	B PENDLEBURY	C.P.P.	17.03.1908
3251	W MANN	C.P.P.	29.11.1913
3253	J W SUTTON	C.P.P.	08.12.1913
3258	H HOPE	LOCOMOTIVE SHUNTER	13.11.1906
3262	J UNSWORTH	STOCKYARD SWEEPER	22.07.1922
3268	J BENNETT	COAL PREP PLANT	22.09.1904
3269	C QUALE	C.P.P.	09.07.1927
3270	W WHALLEY	C.P.P.	04.09.1906
3272	J BUSHELL	C.P.P.	31.03.1907
3277	D NICHOLSON	STORES SERVER	19.04.1936
3278	A TIPPING	ELECTRICIANS MATE	30.12.1936
3280	N BOON	C.P.P.	13.02.1926
3281	J E KENT	C.P.P.	01.05.1921

PAY NUMBER	NAME	OCCUPATION	DATE OF BIRTH
3282	A EVITTS	No 2 PIT BANK FEEDER ATT	10.05.1914
3283	J REYNOLDS	C.P.P.	02.02.1915
3284	J MILLWARD	ROTASIDE TIPPLER	29.12.1910
3285	E C GREENALGH	C.P.P.	20.03.1922
3297	A CORDINGLEY	CLEANER (FEMALE)	30.07.1912
3298	C WOODWARD	GENERAL WORKER	27.03.1909
3305	J HALL	C.P.P.	27.07.1911
3307	A ASPINALL	C.P.P.	02.12.1915
3309	V BAXTER	ASST BANKSMAN	17.05.1912
3312	J STONES	C.P.P.	23.05.1913
3313	F GORE	COAL PREP PLANT	21.11.1904
3314	W WILLIAMS	C.P.P.	05.04.1922
3316	J REDFORD	LAMPMAN	05.02.1910
3318	H COUGHLIN	C.P.P.	07.06.1913
3319	T CHARNOCK	WATCHMAN	26.10.1916
3320	G WHITTLE	C.P.P.	20.12.1925
3323	J HILL	LAMPMAN	09.06.1908
3324	C MORRIS	POINTS OILER (RAILWAYS)	05.03.1915
3326	W HINDLEY	C.P.P.	26.03.1910
3328	K WHITTLE	LOCO SHUNTER	17.10.1934
3332	W PRICE	C.P.P.	02.10.1907
3333	J WHITE	LAMPMAN	26.12.1915
3335	C H NAYLOR	C.P.P.	08.03.1913
3336	F KENNEDY	C.P.P.	14.09.1905
3338	J NAYLOR	C.P.P.	10.09.1910
3339	W CATTERALL	C.P.P.	03.10.1904
3340	E POOLE	C.P.P.	30.05.1927
3341	C NALLY	C.P.P.	23.01.1917
3342	W SLOAN	GENERAL WORKER NIGHTS	24.11.1919
3343	S IWANCYK	C.P.P.	20.01.1910
3344	P WLASIUK	C.P.P.	20.08.1911
3346	D BANCROFT	C.P.P.	16.06.1916
3347	A GRAHAM	C.P.P.	21.09.1929
3349	J CONLAN	C.P.P.	22.10.1909
3351	T SMITH	C.P.P.	10.12.1917
3352	R SIMMS	C.P.P.	17.01.1932
3354	H WHITTLE	GENERAL WORKER	18.12.1909
3356	R MAYOH	C.P.P.	01.12.1925
3357	W BLACKBURN	C.P.P.	01.11.1911
3359	W MARSH	LUBRICATOR No2 ENGINEHOUSE	24.06.1916
3365	E HYDE	ROTASIDE TIPPLER	30.11.1907
3366	L JACKSON	POWDER MAGAZINE ATTENDANT	06.02.1917
3371	R YATES	JUMBO SLINGER	20.10.1913
3372	F McKIERNAN	ACTING ASST BANKSMAN	18.01.1918
3374	L HIGSON	LOCO STOKER	01.07.1928
3376	C MELLING	CHARGEHAND ROTASIDE TIPPLE	26.12.1911
3377	G MOLYNEAUX	LOCOMOTIVE DRIVER	20.11.1920
3384	R RYLANCE	LOCOMOTIVE DRIVER	29.05.1911
3386	J GREGORY	LOCOMOTIVE DRIVER	07.10.1906
3387	R YATES	LOCOMOTIVE DRIVER	18.10.1913
3389	J HALLIWELL	LOCOMOTIVE DRIVER	22.04.1925
3390	A FLITCROFT	TRAFFIC CONTROL	13.06.1935
3392	S MATHEWS	LOCO SHUNTER	19.10.1916
3393	K REDFORD	LOCO SHUNTER	19.09.1926
3394	W McMULLEN	LOCO CLEANER NIGHTS	10.07.1907

PAY NUMBER	NAME	OCCUPATION	DATE OF BIRTH
3465	A FEARICK	BATHS ATTENDANT	18.04.1905
3466	J HOLLAND	BATHS ATTENDANT	09.05.1908
3467	E BATE	BATHS ATTENDANT	08.03.1911
3472	J KINSELLA	BATHS ATTENDANT	18.06.1905
3355	L PARSONS	BATHS ATTENDANT	21.02.1919
3474	F FELL	MEDICAL CENTRE	19.12.1912
3475	H BELSHAW	MEDICAL CENTRE	31.05.1910
3321	P CATTERALL	MEDICAL CENTRE	20.08.1905
3150	K EDWARDS	PLATELAYER	30.09.1920
3153	S COUNCIL	PLATELAYER	08.09.1913
3156	G RATCLIFFE	PLATELAYER	15.11.1915
3157	V KENDRICK	PLATELAYER	30.12.1925
3158	W HUGHES	PLATELAYER	08.12.1924
3160	E SPEAKMAN	PLATELAYER	21.07.1906
3004	F LYTHGOE	SANITARY OFFICER	26.10.1916
3020	H BENTLEY	TUB REPAIRS	18.01.1909
3040	J HASLAM	ASSISTANT BANKSMAN	04.07.1917
3042	A MARSH	COAL PREP PLANT	16.07.1911
3045	G HUNTER	TELEPHONE OPERATOR	17.08.1915
3053	J KELLEHER	MOBILE CRANE SLINGER	28.06.1911
3057	J MADDEN	BANKSMAN	09.02.1915
3062	A JONES	MANAGERS BATMAN	06.11.1910
3070	J WHITTLE	ELECTRICIAN	29.05.1926
3074	J SEDDON	YARD SWEEPER	29.03.1911
3092	P JONES	TUB REPAIRS	13.08.1912
3093	E GREGSON	LAMPMAN	14.06.1909
3100	R PARKINSON	STEAM CRANE SLINGER	23.11.1911
3112	J RAFTRY	C.P.P.	15.12.1912
3115	J CATHERALL	C.P.P.	23.10.1909
3117	J E BRADLEY	BRICKSETTERS MATE	13.12.1910
3118	L MOLYNEAUX	GENERAL WORK	02.02.1918
3119	W H MILLARD	GENERAL WORK	22.01.1916
3121	J GORMLEY	FORK TRUCK LOADER	04.01.1913
3122	J T PIMBLET	C.P.P.	14.09.1919
3123	W HALL	LOCO STOKER	29.08.1908
3127	T S WHITTLE	GENERAL WORK	27.03.1915
3136	E FARRIMOND	LUBRICATOR No 1 PIT BAN	24.01.1913
3152	W JONES	C.P.P.	12.05.1908
3154	A RUSHTON	ELECTRICIAN	03.04.1914
3159	J CORDINGLEY	MAIN LINE WAGON ATT	30.03.1909
3162	J SMITH	GENERAL WORK NIGHTS	11.01.1909
3163	S DANDY	LOCO STOKER	03.08.1910
3168	G TONGUE	ELECTRICIAN	29.06.1931
3170	J HUGHES	ELECTRICIANS MATE	24.10.1905
3172	T MATHEWS	GENERAL WORK	02.06.1908
3181	J DISLEY	OILER No1 ENGINEHOUSE	27.12.1904
3186	J MIDDLEHURST	C.P.P.	02.02.1912
3189	T TAYLOR	ASST BANKSMAN	?

PAY NUMBER	NAME	OCCUPATION	DATE OF BIRTH
3530	W HAWORTH	APPRENTICE ELECTRICIANS	24.01.1953
3531	J W DAVENPORT	MECHANICS AND	09.11.1951
3532	A SEPHTON	TRAINEE MINERS	12.05.1949
3533	J O STYLES	"	02.06.1952
3534	J K EDDINGTON	"	07.06.1952
3535	J K SLATER	"	16.04.1952
3536	D LEVAY	"	05.11.1953
3537	M DAVEY	"	23.05.1952
3539	W MITCHELL	"	20.01.1952
3540	J J COLLINS	"	12.01.1952
3541	I CARTWRIGHT	"	05.07.1950
3542	P LANGHORN	"	08.01.1951
3544	E FARREL	"	15.10.1951
3545	B BAXTER	"	14.06.1952
3546	A PENN	"	14.02.1949
3547	I HEY	"	29.03.1949
3549	M WALSH	"	10.04.1949
3550	D LEWIS	"	19.05.1950
3552	G DALEY	"	20.03.1950
3554	P STEELE	"	28.06.1951
3558	J CARTWRIGHT	"	31.05.1948
3559	J C ROBINSON	"	09.09.1947
3563	B KIERNAN	"	27.06.1950
3573	J GARFIN	"	27.11.1949
3576	W HINDLEY	"	11.05.1951
3580	P RILEY	"	19.06.1950
3581	B HARRISON	"	09.04.1951
3582	M STOKES	"	07.05.1951

Some Facts and Figures

Sinking started 7th May 1908
First coal wound 25th May 1910

Owners   1908 to 1928 The Pilkington Colliery Company
                1928 to 1947 Manchester Collieries
                1947 to 1970 National Coal Board

Shaft depth 890 yards, diameter 21 feet (No 1)

No 1 shaft output 8 tons every 2 minutes

No 1 winding engine 3300 hp

No 1 headgear supplied & erected by Head Wrightson of Stockton on Tees, with the sheaves 98 feet above the ground.

Electricity generation 3000kV

No of Lancashire boilers 16

Pit head baths built 1936

Skip winding (No 2 shaft) installed 1947

Colliery output 2800 tons per day (1967)

Manpower 2,000 at peak

Worst accident 5 men killed by an explosion in June 1939

Winding engines supplied by Yates and Thom, Blackburn

The Lancashire record was achieved in 1967 on the 3-East face in the Worsley four feet seam with an advance of 84ft 2in in one week on the 250yd face.

Closure 3rd April 1970

Appendix.

This book contains the research and information compiled by many people and from many sources. Below is a list of those who have contributed to this publication and other authors whose publications have been used in research. In every case where I am aware of the writer, I freely acknowledge use of their work and have mentioned them below. In those cases where I have been able to contact them I give my thanks for their permission to use their work.

In those cases where I have been unable to contact the contributor I apologise in advance for not consulting with them. If they would care to contact me I will either add their name and reference to this list - or even remove their contribution from the book if this is what they would prefer. As the author receives no royalties for the publication of this book I hope people will not be too offended if their contribution is not acknowledged below or if I have not been able to obtain their prior permission.

My thanks to everyone involved. The names are in no particular order!

Graham Isherwood
Mike Shardlow
Mike Haddon
Len Hudson
J Jones
K Terry
S Farrow
V Keavney
British Coal
Geoffrey Hayes "Collieries and their railways in the Mc/r coalfield"
John Lyon
Ricky Bellamy
The authors of "The Industrial Railways of Bolton, Bury & the Manchester Coalfield" Part 2
The late & much lamented "Lancashire Mining Museum"
Wigan Metropolitan Borough Heritage Centre
"Forward" magazine, Wigan Economic Development.

Industrial Railway Society Newsletter No 172
(http://www.irsociety.co.uk/)
"The sinking of Astley Green Shafts", Transactions, Manchester Geological Society, June 1910
"Abstract of the Coal Mines Act 1911", HMSO
"Modern Practice in Mining", R A S Redmayne, Longmans 1919
"Pithead baths at Astley Green", Carbon Magazine
"Heavy Rope Haulage Installation at Astley Green", TNACM, 1943
"Manchester Collieries Ltd" Newsletters
Steve Leyland
"Manchester Collieries – Technical Report". E H Browne, 19349
"Skip Winding at Astley Green", Colliery Engineering, July 1949
"Pneumatic stowing at Astley Green", TNACM 1951
"Coal Mining Practice", I C F Statham, Caxton, 1958
"Astley Green Colliery" NCB, NW Division, late 50's & Oct 1967
"Fuel Economy from Steam Accumulators", Colliery Engineering, Nov 1953
"Astley Green Colliery", Worsley 5s Face Team Conference, July 1969
Cliff Graham
Wigan Leisure & Culture Trust.